The New
Birdhouse
Book

A HISTORY AND A HOW TO

The New
Birdhouse
Book

A HISTORY AND A HOW TO

**INSPIRATION AND INSTRUCTION
FOR BUILDING 50 BIRDHOUSES**

LESLIE GARISTO

Plans by Ethan Anderson

CRESTLINE

This edition published in 2010 by
CRESTLINE
A division of BOOK SALES, INC.
276 Fifth Avenue Suite 206
New York, New York 10001
USA

This edition published by arrangement with Quarry Books, an imprint of Rockport Publishers, Inc.

ISBN-13: 978-0-7858-2689-7
ISBN-10: 0-7858-2689-0

Design: Leslie Haimes
Cover Images: (clockwise from top left) Maslowski Wildlife
        Productions; © Gwen Berghorn; Courtesy of American
        Primitive; © Rob Gray; © Ira Montgomery; © Rob Gray;
        Mark Hill; Mick Hales. © Robert A. M. Stern Architects

Safety First: This book provides useful instructions, but we cannot anticipate all of your working conditions or the characteristics of your materials and tools. For safety, you should use caution, care and good judgment when following the procedures described in this book. Consider your own skill and the instructions and safety precautions associated with the various tools and materials shown. The publisher cannot assume any damage to property, injury to persons, or losses incurred as a result of misuse of the information provided.

Printed in China
Reprinted in 2010, 2012, 2013

CONTENTS

GIVE THEM SHELTER

No object is more emblematic of domesticity on the one hand, or more representative of our interdependence with wild things on the other, than a birdhouse. Physically it symbolizes all the virtues of home—safety, enclosure, stability; functionally, though, it represents a longing to bring untamed nature into our lives. When we put a bird in a cage, we are exercising our dominion over it. But when we set out a birdhouse, we acknowledge that our lawns, gardens, and backyards

The classic aviary, which first became popular in the late sixteenth century, provides charming housing for birds you wish to keep close to home.

9

can never belong to us alone. The birds, finally, have the right of eminent domain.

Of course, these aren't likely to be among our thoughts when we make the decision to acquire a birdhouse. Indeed, there are probably as many explanations for the appeal of birdhouses as there are birdhouse fanciers. Nevertheless, a few compelling ones stand out.

Since the Renaissance, we have been enamored of miniature houses . . . with the whimsy of barns and cottages and castles no higher than a footstool . . . with tiny chimneys and dormers and cupolas and every imaginable element of human architecture shrunk to sparrow size. Another possible explanation for our love of birdhouses is offered by California folk-art dealer Judy Heidemann: "They make us laugh," she observes.

What could be more charming, after all, than designer Michael Ridel's gray-shingled Cape Cod cottage, with its second-story dormers and hinged front door? What could be wittier than Randy Sewell's all-American diner, complete with red "neon" sign? Or more appealing than a weathered lighthouse that served for decades as a beacon for birds in search of shelter? No wonder that birdhouses, old and new, have emerged as among the most collectible examples of folk art. Many older houses even carry with them mementos of former use—feathers stuck under the eaves, abandoned nests, entry holes pecked smooth by generations of avian inhabitants. Even in an urban living room, a birdhouse reminds us of the freer world *out there*.

While most birdhouses are essentially architectural, many are wild expressions of the quirky personalities who created them. Imagine the now nameless craftsman who fashioned a six-foot birdhouse in the shape of Maine. Or the tinsmith who cut a wren-

Tenements ringing New York City's Clinton Community Garden inspired this very urban birdhouse, designed by conceptual artist Laura Foreman.

The New Birdhouse Book

A vintage house for gregarious martins, crafted in Maine, features forty-eight separate "apartments" for communal living.

size hole in a larger-than-life metal acorn. For decades, most bird-houses were built by dedicated amateurs who loved birds as much as they did their craft. When we rescue a well-used birdhouse from a vine-covered fencepost, or bid on one at a gallery auction, we acknowledge the spirit and creativity of these anonymous artisans.

The Victorians promoted the notion of the yard and garden as an extension of the house itself, as much a living space as the parlor and the dining room—an idea that, happily, has been revived over the past decade. More and more, we look to decorate our gardens as we do our houses, with perennial beds replacing wallpaper and carpeting, and Lutyens benches and Jekyll urns taking the place of sofas and end tables. As objects of charm and beauty, birdhouses have become the most popular of garden ornaments. Like the designs of the gardens themselves, they can be elegant, taking the form of a whitewashed dovecote rising above a bed of Japanese iris, or informal, such as a rustic barrel-shaped birdhouse on whose carved-wood stand clambers a profusion of white clematis. Birdhouses have a host of personalities. They can make us gasp—imagine a sweeping greensward punctuated by a single towering martin house. Just as readily, they can bring smiles, especially such simply lighthearted designs as a wren house fashioned from an old boot in a children's topiary garden. In addition, they add an invaluable deco-

  The New Birdhouse Book

rative dividend, in the form of bright plumage, not to mention brilliant birdsong.

Even if their man-made abodes weren't so appealing, we would surely welcome birds into our yards and gardens. Throughout human history, birds have delighted and fascinated us. Paleolithic artists painted their images onto cave walls in Europe, Africa, and Australia. In various guises, and in numerous cultures, birds were emblems of ancient fertility goddesses. The ancient Egyptians gave their deities the form of birds, from Thoth, the ibis-headed god of knowledge, to the falcon-headed Horus, lord of the sky. Seagoing petrels are often assumed to owe their name to St. Peter, for their apparent ability to walk on water. And bluebirds have long been a symbol of uncomplicated pleasure. There are few sights so charming as one of these lovely birds gently nudging her nestlings out of the birdhouse for their first shaky attempts at flight.

In our urbanized, technological age, many of us are unaware of the beneficial nature of birds. Agricultural societies through the ages, however, have sought to attract birds as an astonishingly effective means of pest control and a ready source of fertilizer. The graceful bluebird is a voracious consumer of beetles, grasshoppers, and caterpillars; sparrows happily gobble up wasps and other winged pests; and owls and kestrels exhibit an unflagging appetite for rats and mice. Praising the owl's prodigious rodent-catching abilities, the nineteenth-century naturalist Charles Waterton wrote, "I have offered it hospitality and protection on account of its persecutions, and for its many services to me." Perhaps the most dramatic example of birdly beneficence took place in Utah in 1848. That was the year horrified Mormon colonists watched their crops being consumed by hordes of crickets; there seemed no way to stem

An architectural birdhouse adds sculptural interest to a country-style china cabinet. Overleaf, a bevy of martin houses dresses up the front yard of a country cottage in Bee, Nebraska.

the destruction until the fortuitous arrival of thousands of hungry gulls, who saved the crops and rescued the Mormons from potential starvation. A monument to the gulls still stands in Salt Lake City.

Egyptian farmers have kept pigeons for centuries in what may be the world's most spectacular birdhouses. The towering mud-and-straw pigeon cotes, which still rise above the Egyptian landscape like monoliths from another world, provide a nearly limitless supply of nutrient-rich fertilizer—an agricultural requisite in a country where three or more crops are reaped every year from the same acreage. Indeed, there was a time when an Egyptian without a pigeon cote could kiss his chances for matrimony goodbye; prospective fathers-in-law regarded him as a man without a future.

Closer to home, those of us struggling to maintain a chemical-free lawn would do well to attract the sparrow, a bird known to gorge itself on weed seeds.

The American naturalist John Muir called birds the "buoys and lighthouses of nature." In their success (or failure) at surviving assaults to the environment, they represent a highly accurate gauge of nature's state of health, warning us of troubles that may still remain unseen and unheeded. One environmental crisis that can no longer be ignored—and the most compelling reason for setting out a birdhouse—is the dramatic loss of habitat that has threatened dozens of species of birds with extinction. The causes are complex and varied: increased use of pesticides by farmers and homeowners, clearing of forest land in the name of development, forestry practices that result in the cutting of hardwoods in favor of faster-growing pine, the pruning of orchards, and the introduction of foreign species. In 1890 and 1891, for example, the American Acclimatization Society, determined to ensure that every bird mentioned in the works of William Shakespeare should flap its wings over American soil, released one hundred European starlings in New York's Central Park. Though the act was well intentioned, today

  The New Birdhouse Book

these prolific and aggressive birds have extended their range throughout virtually all of the contiguous forty-eight states, depriving other, less assertive birds—bluebirds and martins among them—of nesting sites. Over the past century, the eastern bluebird population has quite literally been decimated by loss of habitat.

The erection of birdhouses and nesting boxes can have a dramatic effect. In 1989 Hurricane Hugo ravaged the southeastern coast of the United States, leaving unparalleled destruction in its wake. Among the lesser-known casualties of the storm were 63 percent of the red-cockaded woodpeckers in South Carolina's Francis Marion National Forest. After the deluge, the U. S. Forest Service installed nesting boxes, providing shelter for the birds that had managed to ride out the storm. Two years later the Forest Service counted nearly one thousand woodpeckers in Francis Marion—twice as many, it is believed, as would have survived without the nesting boxes.

Backyard birders, too, can make a difference. Each birdhouse or nesting box erected represents not just the survival of a pair of birds but an opportunity to reproduce and increase the species. It is a simple way of repaying the birds for their countless gifts to us.

So what, ultimately, is a birdhouse? It can be as simple as a recycled detergent bottle, as elaborate as a Bavarian castle in miniature. It might be constructed of bent twigs, old barn wood, or whitewashed cedar. It may look like a Victorian cottage or a railroad car or the Leaning Tower of Pisa. Whatever form it assumes, however, it will always remain a symbol of the beneficence of nature and the extraordinary beauty of birds. With luck, it will also represent the human ability to coexist with and preserve the wild gifts that surround us.

1

BIRDHOUSE BASICS

It's one of those rare days in late winter, when the weather is unseasonably warm and the breeze is full of the smell of spring. Suddenly, it's possible to imagine the world in bloom again and to conjure up the sound of birdsong—just the kind of day that gets people to thinking about putting up a birdhouse or two. Inspired by the balmy weather and the promise of chirping visitors, many of us rush out to satisfy that end-of-winter urge without the least understanding of what

A red, white, and blue "lighthouse" does double duty, providing housing for the birds and gentle entertainment for their human neighbors.

we're buying. No matter how much it pleases us aesthetically, a birdhouse is first and foremost a home for birds. If the house is to be used outdoors, it needs to meet certain standards to be safe for its occupants. And as pretty as your yard may look to *you*, it may not be hospitable to the avian tenants you hope to attract.

To Each Bird a House

The most important thing to know about birdhouses is that different models attract different species of birds, depending on such structural factors as the size of the entrance hole, the depth of the interior, and the height at which the house is mounted or hung. (See the table on page 73 for dimensions and other specifics.)

Don't expect to find a house to suit literally every bird: the only birds that will inhabit man-made houses are cavity nesters—such species as wrens, nuthatches, and starlings, whose natural nesting places are hollow logs or tree limbs. (This still leaves you with upwards of fifty potential species, depending on where you live, as well as the beam nesters.)

The most common commercially produced birdhouses are designed for small birds such as wrens, chickadees, and titmice. Indeed, wrens—the squatters of the bird world—will nest virtually anywhere: old boots and shoes, junked automobile radiators, empty flowerpots, mailboxes, or fishing creels. Wrens have even made their home in a pair of blue jeans left out too long on a laundry line. And wrens are prodigious—some might even say *compulsive*—nest-builders. A male wren may build a half-dozen nests, most of them dummies to dupe or warn off other birds in the area. When the female wren deigns to move in, she often destroys her mate's earnest work, rebuilding the nest to suit her personal fancy.

A tufted titmouse makes its home in this simple but well-constructed house.

  The New Birdhouse Book

Martins in the eastern United States nest mainly in groups. The special features of this vintage two-story martin house—maroon trim and irregularly placed entrance holes—raise it above the ordinary.

Though bluebirds will sometimes nest in houses designed for wrens, it's best to buy a house built to suit their particular needs. (For dimensions of a typical bluebird house, see page 73.) If you're serious about attracting bluebirds—and with the drastic decline in bluebird habitat, everyone who *can* be *should* be—mount the houses four to seven feet off the ground in an open area, preferably at the edge of woodlands (a long fence row is ideal). For each acre or so of land, expect to attract one nesting pair.

Doves, pigeons, and martins generally prefer to nest in colonies. Dovecotes, which attract both doves and pigeons, are traditionally cylindrical, and can range in height from one foot to twelve feet and up. Martin houses usually feature four to twenty-four separate "apartments," though martins will also happily nest in hollowed gourds, massed together and strung from high tree limbs or posts. The gourds should be far enough apart so that a strong gust won't knock them together.

You can also buy houses built specifically for larger birds such as screech, barn, and saw-whet owls, as well as kestrels, flickers, and red-bellied woodpeckers. Wood ducks, too, will nest in man-made houses, especially if you place them near a shallow body of water incorporating islands, snags, and some form of natural cover. To make the duck houses hospitable to their prospective tenants, line the bottom of each cavity with soft debris—wood shavings, soft pine bark, and the like.

A red-shingled wren house at left is suspended from the sturdy branches of a white pine. At right, clay bottles like these have been housing small birds since American Colonial days.

The "porches" ringing this purple martin house, left, keep baby birds from tumbling to the ground. Though it won't attract partridges to the Bradford pear tree at right, a cheerfully painted wren house offers shelter to a variety of small species.

Beam nesters—birds such as phoebes, robins, and barn swallows that typically nest in tree crotches—can be enticed to nest on man-made "shelves." These are generally simple structures, open on two sides, with a shelflike floor and a slanting roof. The particular pleasure of shelf houses derives from their very simplicity and openness: they make it easy to observe the birds' ingenious handi-work—cupped nests plastered together with a mixture of mud and straw—as well as their eventual progeny.

Materials

The best birdhouses are made of wood (cedar, pine, and fir are all good choices), which serves as an excellent insulator and stands up well to the elements. Avoid wood treated with preservatives or insecticides, however. Houses of cement and terra cotta are also generally hospitable to birds, but *never* buy a metal house: it will be

stiflingly hot in summer, and fledglings cannot climb its smooth surface to leave the nest.

Paint is another matter. While birdhouse interiors should always be left unpainted, stained or painted exteriors are fine, as long as the paint is water-based. Common bird lore warns against the use of brightly colored paint, since birds are said to be frightened by vivid colors (the sole exception being martins, who seem to prefer the heat-deflecting quality of white houses). The observations of many backyard birders may refute this claim, however: Georgia artist Randy Sewell, for example, whose colorful birdhouses are fashioned after vernacular roadside architecture, says that local birds flock to his neon-blue diners and crimson fireworks stands. Talk to birders in your area and learn of their observations.

Essentials of Good Construction

No one disputes certain birdhouse basics: specifically, the need for ventilation and drainage. Without proper ventilation, fledglings can suffocate; without drainage, they can drown. Every birdhouse should have at least two holes or slats on either side to allow air to circulate. To keep houses rainproof, the roof should overhang the body of the house by at least one-eighth inch (houses with flat roofs should have shallow rain troughs on two sides). Some kind of overhang to protect birds from sun and rain is also recommended. Another important feature is an interior foothold for babies en route to the great outdoors. A series of cleats or horizontal grooves provides excellent purchase for fledgling feet.

Architect Joseph G. Costa designed his "Subirdian" row houses, left, specifically for downy woodpeckers, whose soft plumage and sweet song still recall for him childhood walks through the woods. The Carpenter Gothic birdhouse at right was designed for wrens and chickadees with a taste for Victoriana.

Scouting a Location

Location is as important as size, shape, height, and construction in the overall birdhouse picture—a truism for birders as well as realtors. In general, a birdhouse should be set away from dense foliage but close enough to such natural perches as trees and shrubs. If you've recently landscaped your property, you may have to change the location of the birdhouse as plantings mature. Orientation is less important, as long as the house is properly designed to deflect rain and sun.

Not all birds prefer to nest in the open, however, and some are extremely picky about their neighborhood. Chickadees and titmice, for example, nest in wooded areas, so their houses should be placed within ten to fifteen feet of dense shrubbery. Purple martins prefer a combination of open fields and water; if you don't have both nearby, the best martin house in the world won't meet this species' standards. Tree swallows, too, nest near bodies of water, such as lakes, ponds, and even swimming pools.

Though houses for smaller birds can be suspended from a branch or beam (or, in the case of gregarious wrens, right from the eaves of your house), larger birdhouses should be mounted on metal or wooden posts set in concrete or a rock-lined hole. Most manufacturers supply information on how to mount their houses, but whatever you do, make sure the mounting is secure; if the house topples, eggs can be smashed and fledglings injured. Some smaller birdhouses are designed to be mounted against a tree. To protect the bark, place a layer of rubber between tree and house.

SAFETY FIRST

In your backyard, as in the wild, predators present a constant danger to baby birds, so houses should be mounted at least five feet from the ground. If cats and squirrels are a problem, try attaching an inverted funnel-shaped piece of metal to the pole, eighteen inches from the ground (the funnel should extend ten inches from the pole on all sides). To hungry raccoons, eggs and baby birds represent a springtime delicacy. Attaching a three-quarter-inch block of wood over the hole—with a hole drilled in the wood to match that of the entryway—will keep nestlings safely away from the reach of even the most rapacious raccoon.

The greatest threat to nesting birds, however, comes not from backyard predators but from other birds. Starlings and many sparrows commonly move in on established birds, sometimes even building their nests on top of the eggs of former inhabitants. If the house you buy comes with an exterior perch, remove it—perches are unnecessary and serve only as an invitation to nest competitors.

TIMING

Flush with enthusiasm, many novice backyard birders eagerly put out their first house, only to find no takers. This doesn't necessarily mean they've done something wrong. It can take several years to attract birds to your birdhouse—many birds, in fact, seem to prefer slightly weathered houses. On the other hand, there may be something amiss. Timing, for example, is extremely important. Though houses can be set out as late as early July in northern climates, the optimum time is early spring, when most migratory birds begin to return to their summer habitats. In North America this means January for the deep South, February for the Middle Atlantic states, and March for the northern United States and Canada. In the British Isles and Europe, February is also the optimal time.

BACKYARD HABITATS

The general habitat your backyard provides is crucial to attracting and maintaining a varied selection of birds. In addition to shelter, all birds require food, water, and cover. If even one of these is absent, you may find yourself the owner of an unoccupied birdhouse. Fortunately, all three are easy to provide.

A bird feeder is the simplest means of providing food, and has the added advantage of showing you exactly which birds will nest in your area. Like houses, feeders don't always attract birds the instant they're set out, but patience will be well rewarded. Placed near a window, a bird feeder provides countless hours of pleasure (around our house, we refer to it as "cat TV"). In late summer, some birds will even bring their young to the feeder with them.

Nuthatches, chickadees, finches, and titmice prefer hanging feeders, while sparrows, towhees, doves, and cardinals like to feed on the ground. Since birds aren't the neatest of diners, normal spillage will usually satisfy ground feeders. You might also set out a basket or a shallow dish with drainage holes. By far the most popular food for the widest variety of birds is sunflower seeds, but cracked corn and mixed seed are favorites as well. Insect-eaters such as woodpeckers are attracted to suet, peanut butter, and bird cakes; there are many fine suet feeders on the market, but a mesh bag, such as the kind used for onions, mounted to a tree trunk will work just as well. It's best to avoid bread as a staple, since it's low in essential nutrients and is metabolized too quickly to provide energy to fight the cold. It's also been known to attract unwanted rodents.

Before feeders, of course, birds depended on nature to provide them with sustenance, often in the form of fruit-, seed-, and nut-bearing trees, shrubs, vines, and flowers. Some of the best natural sources of bird food are dogwoods, for their autumn fruit; berry bushes of all kinds, including sumacs; flowering crab apple; sunflowers and burning bush, for their seeds; and, especially, Virginia creeper, a prolific vine whose fruit attracts dozens of species of birds.

Trees and shrubs also provide perches and natural cover. For additional cover, set out your Christmas trees rather than consigning them to landfill. And consider keeping a corner of your yard "wild"—far from meticulous, birds prefer a little mess, in the form of brush piles, dead tree limbs, and tangled weed patches.

If your yard lacks a natural source of water, a birdbath is inexpensive, attractive, and eminently practical. Set it up in an open area, but make sure that a perch of some kind is no more than ten feet away. In warmer weather, birds are especially fond of drip-baths, which can be as simple as a water-filled pail with a small hole in the bottom, hung above the birdbath.

Don't forget, too, that birds need an abundance of nest materials. Each spring, provide them with nesting materials—yarn, cotton, pet and human hair, straw, grass, twigs, strips of paper or cloth, feathers, down, bark, moss, even cellophane. Make sure, however, that no strand is longer than about four inches; birds can entangle themselves in longer strands. You can simply leave these raw materials out in the open, or buy or improvise a box for them. Mount it near a window and you guarantee yourself the fun of watching an avian architect at work.

WINTER CLEANUP

Having enjoyed your birdhouse all spring and summer, you'll wake one day to an autumnal chill and the sight of turning leaves. The nesting season ends by late fall, even for nonmigratory birds, and this is the time for birdhouse maintenance. An essential feature of any birdhouse is a removable wall, floor, or roof for easy cleaning. (If you're lucky enough to have martins, make sure the houses are mounted on poles that can be lowered.) Take out old nests and debris, and scrub the interior with a stiff brush. If parasites are present, use strong soap and water and rinse well. Avoid insect spray unless absolutely necessary.

To keep nature's ravages to a minimum, bring the house indoors if you can. This is a good time to make repairs and to repaint, if

The quintessential martin
house, painted a traditional
white, rises like a beacon
above a rural farmhouse.

31

either is called for. If the house will be wintering outside, cover the hole to discourage mice from taking up residence.

Don't forget to keep the feeder well stocked. Overwintering birds such as chickadees and titmice need the extra food now more than they did when the days were long and balmy, and they'll be more likely to inhabit your birdhouses come spring if you provide them with winter sustenance. Another way to encourage birds to stick around is to provide them with a roosting box, a large houselike structure with interior roosts for a number of birds.

Well cared for, a birdhouse can be a perennial source of pleasure and discovery. Like many backyard birders, however, you may find that one isn't enough. If you have room for more, by all means indulge your enthusiasm: your family and neighbors won't complain, and the birds will sing your praises.

A rustic feeder not only adds beauty to the winter garden, but helps support dozens of species of overwintering birds.

2

RUSTIC ABODES

Every birdhouse, no matter what its design, possesses an element of rusticity. Strip it of its architectural finery and you have a structure that was designed to live—and support life—in nature. Given a few years' use and exposure to the elements, even the most elegant architectonic birdhouse begins to take on the patina of the out-of-doors. Sun and rain blister its paint, revealing the natural wood beneath. Birds smooth the contours of its entrance hole as they come and go. Bits of

The charm of a simple wooden birdhouse, mounted against an old tree, is enhanced by the twinings of wisteria.

The creative sleight-of-hand of Alabama's Reverend Benjamin Franklin Perkins turns a simple gourd house, left, into a small work of art. Center, an ethereal bent-twig birdhouse, crafted by furniture designer Clifton Monteith, seems ready to take wing. The basic vintage house at right has a slightly dilapidated but comfortable quality.

nesting material find their way into cracks and crevices. What was once the perfect replica of an eighteenth-century mansion now looks like the home for wild things that it was intended to be.

Given their predilection for the natural look, the birds undoubtedly prefer it that way. Perhaps that's why some of the most successful birdhouses are rustic by design. Incorporating natural, often weathered, materials, rustic birdhouses most closely resemble the wild homes of cavity-nesting birds, such as tree trunks and hollow logs.

Basic Boxes

The most basic rustic houses are simple stand-ins for what nature no longer provides in sufficient abundance. Thanks largely to the efforts of such wildlife advocates as the National Audubon Society and local natural history societies, plain boxes of cedar and pine now dot the landscape from southern Florida to the Pacific Northwest, housing birds whose habitats have been severely reduced by development and deforestation. The North American Bluebird Society, for example, has done enormous work in spreading their message: without human intervention, the beautiful Eastern bluebird will most likely vanish from fields and backyards forever. Delaware's celebrated Winterthur Museum maintains twenty-five cedar-shingled bluebird houses in their sprawling gardens, with spectacular results—now the lilting call of bluebirds wafts above the copses of azalea and rhododendron all spring and summer long.

Other successful rustic "housing projects" include boxes for owls, kestrels, and wood ducks. Because they feed on rodents and large insects, both owls and kestrels are important allies in the pest-control war, and are a good deal safer than chemical pesticides. Communities across North America have set out hundreds of the spacious boxes to help fight rodent infestations. (One of the most publicized uses of owl boxes was in New York's Central Park, where the rat population was booming in spite of repeated applications of poison; unfortunately, the attractive owl boxes proved too strong a temptation to human city dwellers, and most of them were stolen before the owls could get a foothold.)

Though vegetarian wood ducks won't do much in the area of vermin control, the presence of these elegant birds—the most colorful ducks in North America—is sufficient justification for setting out a duck house or two, if the environment is hospitable (see page 73). They may be migratory, but wood ducks are home-bodies at heart: a female wood duck will return to the same area—and very likely the same house—year after year.

Handcrafted in England, the charming thatched-roof birdhouse at top evokes classic Celtic wattle-and-daub architecture. Bottom, a rough-hewn bluebird house from the American Primitive collection takes its name literally.

Organic Architecture

No one knows for sure what the earliest birdhouses looked like, but they were probably functional affairs, built of natural, unfinished materials. Their builders' intent was certainly less aesthetic than practical; people living in close harmony with nature know that there exists no better means of insect control than a clutch of songbirds. On the North American continent, the first birdhouses were probably hollowed-out gourds, strung from trees and poles by Native Americans of the Southeast to attract purple martins. When the European settlers arrived, they took up the practice, and it continues to this day, especially in the rural South. Hung together by the dozens, these gourd houses are still intended to house

The basic bluebird house at left is equipped with a baffle to foil potential predators. Center and right, a thatched-roof coconut and a hollowed log provide organic shelter for small birds. At far right, gourds grouped to attract martins take on a pleasing, sculptural aspect.

  The New Birdhouse Book

Michael Ridel's "Wood Shed" has the appeal of a hand-hewn country homestead.

nesting martins, but they also attract other small birds, including titmice, bluebirds, nuthatches, swallows, house sparrows, flycatchers, and wrens.

The tradition of gourd houses has weathered the centuries because the gourds suit their purpose perfectly. But the houses also possess natural charm: a single gourd, strung from an overhead branch, has an almost whimsical quality; strung in groups, they take on the look of modern sculpture. Indeed, in the hands of artists like Alabama's Reverend Benjamin Franklin Perkins, they *are* works of art. A self-taught painter and preacher, Reverend Perkins decorates his "churches for the birds" with patriotic and religious motifs, including flags, the Statue of Liberty, and bits of writing, all in a striking palette of red, white, and blue. Though highly embellished, the gourds reflect a reverence for nature that keeps them well in the realm of the rustic.

Traditional Rustics

While some European immigrants to North America were setting out hollow gourds like their tribal neighbors, others fashioned bird bottles of glazed clay. The small bottles were fixed to the clapboards of colonial houses and provided hospitable shelter to wrens and other gregarious birds. (They continue to attract feathered tenants even today in Virginia's Colonial Williamsburg.) Other basic houses were fashioned from weathered barrels and buckets. Aarne Anton, a New York dealer in American folk art, found a particularly compelling barrel-house in Elmira, New York. Built in the state penitentiary in the early part of this century, the house is purely functional save for a painted finial of turned wood on the top. Even thus unadorned, it undoubtedly brought a small element of freedom to the dark confines of the prison.

The Nesting Instinct

Some rustic houses are modeled not after logs or tree trunks but the nests woven inside of them. Basket birdhouses have been an important part of the southern handicraft tradition for generations, and they can still be found nailed to fenceposts and barn sidings throughout the South. Woven skeps—traditionally used to house colonies of bees—were also modified to make charming birdhouses, a trend being revived by the firm Country Originals.

Malcolm Wells, a Cape Cod architect with a special interest in birdhouses, has designed a "living" birdhouse—a wooden nesting shelf covered with a mound of topsoil, compost, and mulch, and surrounded by twigs, grasses, and blooming wildflowers. The most "natural" of rustic birdhouses, it derives its inspiration from the birds' own unique architecture.

Taking their cue from the "plaster" houses built by robins and swallows, German "wood-crete" birdhouses are made, as their name suggests, from a combination of wood and concrete. Hung from a branch or fixed to the trunk of a tree, they have a rough "make-do" charm that belies the efficiency (and bird-friendliness) of their construction.

Rustic by Design

In the realm of birdhouse architecture, as in contemporary design in general, rustic doesn't necessarily connote simple or unadorned. A whole generation of designers are creating rustic birdhouses that

The New Birdhouse Book

deftly blend utility and beauty. Reflecting a growing environmental awareness, these designers not only use natural materials, they often put cast-off materials to new use. Recycling, in fact, has long been a traditional element of birdhouse construction; for years, local folk artists have used old barn wood, discarded license plates, and other found objects to create unique pieces of avian architecture. (More examples of this type of design can be found in Chapter Four, "Fanciful and Fantastic.")

Randy Ouzts, who once designed windows for Gucci and Bergdorf Goodman in New York, now turns out extraordinary rustic birdhouses in his North Carolina studio. While his basic raw material isn't recycled per se, it was, until recently, considered worse than trash by most of his southern neighbors: Ouzts's elegant birdhouses and feeders are fashioned of kudzu, the prodigious vine that is literally engulfing the southern United States in its twisted

Whimsical details of rural architecture inspired these birdhouses from the design firm Garden Source. On each model roofs, windows, portals, and chimneys are harmonized to create a miniature replica of the real thing.

tendrils. Woven into a birdhouse, kudzu is transformed from a vegetable pest into something ethereal and surprisingly nestlike, and birds find it uniquely hospitable.

Sam and Pat Grove, husband-and-wife designers in Spicewood, Texas, construct whimsical and architectural rustic birdhouses from cedar trees felled by local developers. Everything on the houses, including architectural flourishes, was at one time destined for the landfill—driftwood, bits of fencing wire removed from neighboring ranches, cans scavenged from the trash of a local school cafeteria. Birds' nests being the apotheosis of found art, the Groves' designs seem particularly appropriate to their function.

The wild and whimsical birdhouses sold at Growingthings, in Brooklyn, New York, might have been decorated by delirious robins: their fanciful ornamentation includes acorns, balls from the sweet-gum tree, and pine cones. Larry Kenosha's graceful birdhouse is woven of native Minnesota basswood and trimmed with local red willow; bits of sawn popple stick give it the look of an otherworldly log cabin. A Native American, Kenosha learned from a tribal elder to gather materials with respect; one night in a dream he saw his birdhouse, and after two years of architectural refinements, it found its way to such citadels of retail design as New York's Whitney Museum Shop.

In southern England, the artisans of English Thatch turn out some of the most enchanting rustic birdhouses ever to grace a country garden or suburban backyard. Made with authentic Devon thatch, the houses have a rough-hewn architectural charm, incorporating such features as the traditional "English eyebrow" arch.

Perhaps the most extraordinary rustic birdhouses come from the hand of Michigan furniture designer Clifton Monteith. Crafted mostly of bent willow and cedar, the birdhouses are highly sculptural, each incorporating a complex series of planes and curves. A Monteith birdhouse readily brings to mind the grace of birds in

The New Birdhouse Book

flight—though in fact, most of his houses go to collectors who keep them safely away from real birds and the out-of-doors.

Nevertheless, rustic birdhouses have a special affinity for wooded landscapes and countrified backyards. The same birch-log house that adds charm to the shaded porch of a lakeside cabin seems right at home hanging from the eaves of a suburban toolshed. And because they blend naturally with the landscape, rustic birdhouses don't need to stand alone. If a yard is large enough, dozens of them can decorate tree trunks, fence posts, even the sides of outbuildings.

Not every environment can support a towering cluster of martin-house gourds on twenty-foot poles, but a half-dozen gourds, suspended from the spokes of a recycled wagon wheel, make for instant sculpture even in a garden of modest proportion. And wooded or not, there is no yard so small that it couldn't accommodate the charm of a single diminutive woven wren house. The wrens, if they could, would certainly agree.

3

ARCHITECTURAL OPTIONS

Over the years, birdhouses have assumed every conceivable form, from simple wooden boxes bereft of decoration to human figures whose open mouths served as entrance holes, to futuristic plastic "yo-yos," designed in the early 1960s to complement modern architecture. But one trend has remained constant: when we build for the birds, more often than not, *house* is where the heart is. Attribute it to anthropomorphism, or the gentle sense of whimsy that birds

But for its scale, this shuttered mansion, complete with cupola and widow's walk, might have been built for the family of a Nantucket sea captain.

Dating from 1866, this architectural birdhouse wonder, above, was forged by the Miller Iron Works of Providence, Rhode Island. The cast-iron form ensured its survival well beyond the nineteenth century. Also built to endure, a stalwart dovecote—once the ultimate status symbol—lends distinction to an English garden, right.

seem to inspire, but the vast majority of birdhouses have always taken their architectural cue from human habitations.

Dovecotes and Martin Houses

As early as the thirteenth century, Europeans were building architectural birdhouses on a grand scale. From the late Middle Ages through the early Victorian era, the predominant European birdhouse was the dovecote, a cottage-size structure, usually of stone, built to house the pigeons that were a staple of the European diet. (Some surviving cotes are so large that they have been comfortably converted to house people.) Like the ancient dovecote at Athelhampton, England, and the two eighteenth-century pigeon houses built for the Parlange plantation in southern Louisiana, many were simple rounded stone structures with conical roofs—the traditional "pepper-pot" shape.

In the nineteenth and early twentieth centuries, dovecotes were generally downsized to suit smaller, middle-class gardens, but they still retained some distinctive architectural features. The British garden designer Gertrude Jekyll, a former painter, did much to

promote the dovecote as garden ornament not just for the wealthy, but for the average citizen. J. P. White's Pyghtle Works of Bedford, England, supplied decorative dovecotes to bird fanciers around the world, and the company's charming catalogue illustrations are emblematic of the prevailing styles in dovecote and garden design: an oak barrel with a conical shingled roof marks the pathway in a country garden; a stately rectangular pigeon cote with its lead-covered mansard-style roof stands sentry over the manicured hedges of a formal landscape in the French style.

Just as dovecotes had their beginnings in rural, agricultural settings, so did martin houses. Unlike the pigeons who resided in traditional dovecotes, however, martins weren't valued as food or fertilizer producers, but as highly efficient insectivores; one purple martin may consume as many as 250,000 mosquitoes and other insects in a single season, reason enough for any farmer to put up a martin house or two. The basic martin house looks a bit like a typical midwestern farmhouse: a multistoried white building with a pitched roof and numerous "windows" opening onto individual nesting compartments. (In the eastern United States, martins prefer to nest en masse, but their cousins in the deserts of the Southwest remain solitary nesters. In the Pacific Northwest the martins eschew birdhouses to nest in large colonies on cliffs.) Perhaps the most extraordinary example of martin housing can be found in Griggsville, Illinois, the self-proclaimed martin capital of the world. In the center of town rises a martin skyscraper with room for six hundred or so of the well-loved migrants.

Architect George F. Henschel found the model for his painted-wood birdhouse in the Bedford, New York, Free Library building, built in 1807—whose renovation, not coincidentally, he shepherded.

  The New Birdhouse Book

Elements of Style

Birdhouses have been in vogue since the sixteenth century, but they reached their height of expression during the Victorian era—an age marked by its celebration of the domestic virtues and an unprecedented enthusiasm for the idea of *home*. From the nineteenth century on, birdhouse architects turned out thousands of miniature residences, some primitive, others nearly palatial.

Typical of folk art, architectural birdhouses were constructed of whatever materials could be scrounged or put to reuse, such as old crates and barrels, toothpicks, Popsicle sticks, and wood pulled from abandoned barns or tumbledown fences. Architectural and other details might be provided by chunks of broken glass, soda-pop caps, wooden guitar picks, balls of tinfoil, glitter or sand (for rooftop snow), or paint. In the collection of New York's American Primitive Gallery is a red-and-white cabin birdhouse whose "logs" were fashioned entirely from wooden fishing lures.

Even the most basic architectural houses featured some kind of loving detail, whether it was a row of scalloped shingles on an otherwise plain wood roof, a small whittled chimney, or windows and doors painted in a rainbow palette. Many birdhouses, of course, were as elaborate as the full-scale architecture that inspired them. Victorian domiciles, loaded with gingerbread, were especially popular and continue to be; an ornate Victorian-style birdhouse in the American Primitive collection was made in this century by Chippewa Indians, whose models may have been the houses of Scandinavians who settled near the reservation in the late 1800s. Other Victorian-style birdhouses found their inspiration

Despite its metropolitan roots, Joyce Olsen's "Brooklyn Brownstone," left, seems very much at home in a lush garden setting. At right, a shady verandah and gingerbread trim invite birds and their admirers to this charming avian summerhouse.

The New Birdhouse Book

Birdhouses have been fashioned after every conceivable human edifice, from Victorian Gothic cottages to quaint country churches to pillared municipal buildings—all of which make an appearance in the not-so-urban sprawl exhibited in this roadside display.

in patterns printed in popular magazines and newspapers from the 1920s on; though surviving examples share nearly identical architecture, most have been distinctively personalized with paint, trim, and appliqués.

Regional Designs

More modest houses, too, served as the creative spark for birdhouse builders. Many birdhouses were small-scale recreations of local architecture or specific buildings. A white "saltbox" birdhouse built in Maine in the 1940s boasts a painted-brick foundation and chimneys, a shingled roof, red-painted trim, and a matching red-and-white fence; it is the very model of a New England house of the period. A permanent fixture in Jean Voight's shop, Dovetails, is a large birdhouse bearing the distinctive architectural details of Virginia's Eastern Shore. Indeed, birdhouses come in as many architectural styles as the human habitations that inspired them— Adirondack split-log lodges, squat southwestern-style "adobe" houses, San Francisco Victorians as lacy and lush as wedding cakes.

In my own New Jersey neighborhood stands a wonderful, slightly ramshackle Victorian house with a gabled roof and a spacious wraparound porch; before you reach the front steps, you find yourself seeing double, in the form of a miniature version of the same house. The most distinctive difference, aside from scale, arises from the tufts of straw protruding from the tiny "doorway." Such architectural replicas were common among the house-proud Victorians as well as their twentieth-century descendants. But other birdhouse builders chose grander, more public homes for their models: replicas of the White House and Thomas Jefferson's Mon-

Drawing on the English tradition of agricultural architecture, John P. Meyer designed his "Wrenpost" to be in harmony with its environment.

ticello have provided shelter to generations of birds regardless of political persuasion. One artisan—perhaps a recent immigrant still harboring poignant memories of his homeland—modeled a martin house after the Leaning Tower of Pisa.

The architectural urge didn't end with houses, of course. Birdhouses more often than not were built by country dwellers, and they reflected the full gamut of rural architecture—barns, silos, country churches, lighthouses. Judy Heidemann, whose California shop, Wild Goose Chase, specializes in folk-art houses of all kinds, remembers with great fondness a farm-birdhouse consisting of barn, silo, and a farmhouse modeled after the farmer's own.

Their country pedigree notwithstanding, architectural birdhouses were by no means limited to the rural. Folk art has always been distinguished by the fertile imaginations of its practitioners, and birdhouse art is no exception. One New England martin house was modeled after an elaborate Bavarian castle, with Gothic tracery, carved-wood turrets, and a bell tower with a tiny working bell.

Contemporary Trends

Today, as in the nineteenth century, birdhouse designers continue to find inspiration in domestic architecture. Sam Scovil, Jr., of Maine's Backshore Woodworks, builds elegantly streamlined birdhouses that are, first and foremost, for the birds; like many a contemporary architect, his priorities are safety, comfort, and beauty, in that order. Though his birdhouses don't try to mimic human architecture, they take their lacy, gingerbread look from the scrolled porches of New England Victorians. Similarly, the Streck family of New Mexico look to the Tex-Mex architecture of towns like Taos and Chimayo for the painted tin and copper details that ornament their wooden birdhouses.

Combining a lifelong fascination with architecture and antiques, artist Michael Ridel creates architectural birdhouses distinguished by the elegance and intricacy of their detailing. He built his first birdhouse after a friend tore down a fifty-year-old fence and offered it to him as firewood. Ridel was entranced by the beautiful, weathered look of the wood, and decided then and there that it would *not* be used for burning. He continues to use recycled materials for his birdhouses—old wood, rusted hinges, glue rather than nails. Turning strictly to American architecture for inspiration, he is especially fond of his Shaker-style birdhouses; the Shakers' extraordinary sense of proportion imbues even these breadbox-size miniatures with a characteristic grace and beauty.

A different kind of grace infuses the unique birdhouses of Lady Slipper Designs. For nearly two decades, the not-for-profit Minnesota co-op has created striking birdhouses from native kiln-dried pine. The houses, painted a reflecting white, resemble architectural prototypes, ranging in style from Victorian and Greek Revival to Georgian and Beaux Arts.

From Bauhaus to Birdhouse

Architectural birdhouses are by no means mired in the previous century. Atlanta, Georgia, artist Randy Sewell finds his inspiration in the quirky roadside buildings that were a part of his peripatetic childhood. Family auto trips took him to places like Dogland and the Reptile Farm; as tourist attractions they were inevitably less exciting than their exotic names, but as architectural inspiration they had staying power. Today Sewell-housed birds nest in, among other places, Crazy Eddie's Fireworks Stand, the Checkerboard Diner, a wood-and-wire Muffler House, and the Reptile Farm of

Laura Foreman's New York City tenement-inspired birdhouse offers multistory habitation for city and country birds alike.

earlier days. Sewell has a special touch for the details that give these buildings their tacky charm. His Foot-Long Hot Dog House, for instance, is topped by a painted-wood wiener and accompanying ruler, with the Os in Hot Dog serving as twin entrance holes.

Frank Lloyd Wright, who had a lifelong interest in garden ornament, may or may not have designed a birdhouse or two during his career. If he did, he would be part of a time-honored tradition; Stanford White and Charles Platt, among other architects, found the design of dovecotes and birdhouses a pleasant diversion from the rigors of traditional architecture. Contemporary architects, too, have tried their hand at birdhouse design. In a 1987 show at the Parrish Museum in Southampton, New York, architectural luminaries such as Michael Graves and Robert A. M. Stern offered up a striking variety of modern and postmodern avian abodes. Graves's coyly titled Christopher's Wren House is the essence of Postmodernism, with its updated tip of the hat to Greek and Romanesque architecture. William B. White's Total Aviary Environment is the Guggenheim Museum shrunk to sparrow proportions.

The best architectural birdhouses combine a love of design with a reverence for nature, leavened with a good dose of wit. Certainly, Robert A. M. Stern drew on that wit when he designed his postmodern Owl-i-gorical House, as did the anonymous New England artisan who constructed a wildly swaybacked storybook house during the depths of the Great Depression. By reducing architectural design to an avian scale, birdhouse designers create structures that add a whimsical note to the outdoor landscape—and remind us that we humans are not alone in our search for comfortable shelter.

The whitewashed birdhouses from Lady Slipper Designs emphasize purity of architectural form. Here, a Greek revival–style church offers avian sanctuary.

4

FANCIFUL AND FANTASTIC

In Moscow's State Historical Museum stands a peasant couple, their outstretched arms frozen in time, their mouths agape and their eyes wide with what strikes the observer as amused pleasure. Perhaps that amusement derives from the couple's secret identity—they are, in reality, a pair of folk-art birdhouses in disguise, whose hollow heads once sheltered nesting starlings and their hungry broods. Carved a century ago by peasant craftsmen, the wooden figures

Whitey's Fish Campstore, set among the bushes, was obviously designed by an enthusiastic fisherman for his avian tenants.

Randy Sewell's eye-catching birdhouses pay homage to the quirky roadside architecture of bygone and fast-disappearing American highways.

represent a long tradition of amateur woodworking in Russia, where forest land was—and continues to be—abundant, and where wood has always been a natural medium for artistic expression.

Birdhouses to Go

Unlike serious architects, the builders of birdhouses have never been hemmed in by zoning regulations, architectural traditions, or considerations of taste and community standards—much to the joy of the builders and their admirers. Though birdhouses are by nature functional, their forms have more often than not been fanciful, reflecting the hobbies, philosophies, and preoccupations of their creators. From the nineteenth century on, one popular theme has been transportation: birdhouses have taken the form of boats, trains, and, beginning in the twentieth century, automobiles and airplanes. The American Primitive collection boasts a trolley and a Chesapeake & Ohio caboose, the latter with such authentic details as movable wheels. Also in the collection are two planes: one is a small-scale but accurate replica of the real thing; the other—typical of folk art—is a wild embellishment on the *idea* of airplane: a towering split-level flying machine with propeller, portholes, and a large running-horse weathervane. Such whimsies were designed not just as shelter for the birds but as decorative, one-of-a-kind lawn ornaments. In the realm of the birdhouse, boats, too, can be true to form or fabulous—from a classic 1930s ocean liner to a fanciful Noah's ark, complete with animals. For bellicose birds, contemporary artist Randy Sewell has even fashioned an ironclad Monitor.

Witty and Whimsical

A common theme, among artists in general and birdhouse builders in particular, is the human or animal form. But while many, perhaps most, artists have approached these forms with reverence, birdhouse architects are clearly drawn to them for the inevitable humor arising from the oddball juxtaposition of form and function. Lee Steen, a Montana craftsman, created dozens of carved-wood birdhouses in the shape of human heads before his death in the 1970s; the birds happily came and went through eye sockets and open mouths.

Contemporary wood-carver Barry Leader carries on the tradition in his Pennsylvania studio. Leader's wooden birdhouses, painted in shockingly vibrant colors, are pure whimsy: a black-and-white cow with flared nostrils, three-dimensional eyelashes, and horns rising atop a peaked roof; a bewhiskered cat with protruding snout; and a "bird house" that is quite literally that—complete with outstretched wings and cartoon-variety legs. In a similar mode, architects James Righter and Kimo Griggs designed a painted-wood bluebird house for the 1987 Parrish Museum show that took off on the idea of "bird"; it featured a highly stylized beak-perch atop a pair of spindly six-foot legs.

Pure Fantasy

Many birdhouses simply defy classification, reflecting the unique imaginative gifts of their creators; long before "serious" art embraced the abstract and the free-form, folk artists were unselfconsciously turning out wildly abstract objects, birdhouses among them. A rectangular red, white, and blue birdhouse, found in Iowa and probably dating from the 1930s, features a trio of entrance holes that can be closed with movable slats; on each slat is painted a weird, unblinking eye. Another vintage house, dating from around the same period, looks like a wild interpretation of

Vivid colors and flamboyant forms distinguish a fanciful wren house from Arts for the Birds.

The New Birdhouse Book

L. Frank Baum's Emerald City, a crazy turreted admixture of futurism and Aztec architecture.

Some of the most strikingly original birdhouses have been wrought by self-taught "outsider" artists of the American South, men and women with no formal schooling in the artistic traditions who have nevertheless created works as inspired and exciting as anything that ever hung on museum walls. Willie Massey, for example, was a Kentucky folk artist—in his own words a "trickster"—known for his boldly painted and wildly ornamented avian sculptures and birdhouses. He was a master of the found object: his birdhouses are adorned with birds, snakes, and satellites wrought from fruit crates, twigs, aluminum foil, scrap metal, and whatever else was at hand.

Alabama artist Mose Tolliver, on the other hand, embellishes his birdhouses with paint alone. Indeed, Tolliver uses the birdhouses, which are built by his son, as canvases on which he fashions arresting primitive paintings of birds and other animals; with their stark two-dimensionality, they recall the Paleolithic cave paintings of Lascaux and Altamira.

The Birdhouse as Art

In an age of increasing environmental awareness, birdhouses have themselves become the *subject* of art, as well as vehicles for a host of political, philosophical, and environmental viewpoints. In 1990, Wisconsin's Charles A. Wustum Museum of Fine Arts invited artists from all over to use the bird dwelling as an artistic point of departure, and the results ranged from the wry (Harriete Estel

Arts for the Birds created a birdhouse that truly deserves the name, top, and a fetching canine-faced coop, middle. At bottom, the inspiration for this vintage birdhouse of carved and painted wood must surely have been pure fantasy.

Two folk-art birdhouses from the American Primitive collection are designed in a "future Gothic" style unlikely to be seen in the realm of human architecture.

Berman's steel-and-wood houses "papered" with commercial cookie and cracker wrappers) to the unsettling (Jon Sontag's architectural Bird Mausoleum: Renaissance Model, with its life-size effigy of a deceased bird at the entry hole). Some of the houses in the exhibit appear fragile enough to decompose at any moment; others are menacing, barbed with spikes or thorns. They speak alternately of a supremely delicate environment and a terrifying threat to the natural world. Richard C. Newman's Bird Soul Catcher Monument is a totemic cross-shaped structure adorned with collaged images of skulls and masks, as frightening as it is beautiful.

No other contemporary artist has so thoroughly explored the

birdhouse theme as Laura Foreman. Her obsession with birdhouses began innocently enough, as she sat one afternoon in a vest-pocket park in the New York City neighborhood of TriBeCa. Like so many other neighborhoods in the city, TriBeCa, with its low rents and spacious warehouses, had once attracted artists, but as it gradually succumbed to gentrification, the artists were forced out. Looking around at the small patch of green, Foreman wondered if the birds, too, would soon find themselves homeless. It was then that she hatched an idea to design a series of birdhouses for the park, dedicated to the artists who had moved on. Alas, she was unable to find funding for the project, but it helped spark a new artistic direction. She has since created five site-specific birdhouses for New York City parks, including a Funky Birdhouse for the low-rent Lower East Side. Cobbled together with bits and pieces of demolition flotsam, it offers shelter to city-dwelling sparrows.

Her passion is clearly shared by scores of birdhouse builders, past and present, who have found in the form a unique expression of that ineffable quality we call the human imagination. Some have been motivated by humor, others by a sense of appreciation for nature, and still others by the need to express an opinion. Together, they have helped to lift birdhouse architecture out of the realm of the functional and elevate it to something as wondrous as the winged creatures who inhabit their creations.

Fanciful birdhouses can be streamlined and modern or appealingly kitschy. From Arts for the Birds, a wild green columnar house and a cuckoo clock for wrens, top, are more at home indoors than out. Bottom, Laura Foreman scavenged demolition sites for the components of her Funky Birdhouse, which now graces a New York City park.

5
COLLECTING AND DISPLAYING

You're at a flea market, or browsing the aisles of a rural antiques shop, and you spot it: a weathered old birdhouse that instantly brings to mind childhood summers in the country, the surprise of a blue robin's egg, languid afternoons filled with the scent of honeysuckle and the sound of birdsong. It's at that moment that you become a collector, forever under the spell of houses with thumbnail-size windows and barns no bigger than a bread box. Suddenly, you find

A striking architectural birdhouse—complete with dormer windows and portal—offers pleasant contrast to the formal neoclassic mirror above it.

yourself entranced by peeling paint and crumbling clapboard, and your heart quickens at the sight of bird scratches and swallow droppings. You can take comfort, of course, in the knowledge that you're not alone in your mania for these microdwellings. Birdhouses are increasingly valued as collectibles and one-of-a-kind examples of folk art.

Unfortunately—and inevitably—as demand has grown, so have prices. Though old birdhouses can still be found for reasonable amounts, many sell at exorbitant prices, with extraordinary examples sometimes carrying four-figure price tags. And the booming market for old birdhouses has spawned a host of reproductions, many of them crafted of recycled materials, and carefully "weathered" to take on the look of age. More than ever, then, the successful collector needs to know where to look, what to look for, and how much to pay for it.

Determining Value

New and reproduction birdhouses can be found almost everywhere, from chic housewares boutiques to department store chains to mail order catalogues. If authenticity isn't a priority, there's no reason to turn your nose up at these new, and often reasonably priced, houses—especially if you intend to use them out-of-doors. In addition, a host of talented craftspeople are carrying on the birdhouse tradition; though their creations may not see an immediate or exponential increase in value, these collectibles in their own right could very well appreciate over the years. The birdhouses of designers such as Randy Sewell, Michael Ridel, and Clifton Monteith are small pieces of contemporary art, and like the older birdhouses that inspired them, many are one of a kind.

The best way to recognize a stand-out birdhouse, new or old, is to familiarize yourself with what's out there. Steven Shapiro, whose Newmarket, Maryland, antiques shop specializes in birdhouses and other folk-art collectibles, advises collectors to look for unusual houses or those exhibiting a high degree of craftsmanship; no matter how old, he warns, common examples are going to remain common. Especially valuable are handmade touches: porches, pillars, chimneys, weathervanes, painted shrubbery, movable parts, houses embedded with buttons or bits of colored glass. Rather than detracting from a piece's value, weathering—chipped or worn paint, rusted nails, wood that's been gently warped by time and the elements—and evidence of use enhance collectibility. According to Susie Fisk-Stern, whose Ridgefield, Connecticut, shop sells old and new birdhouses, the most popular models are architectural and highly detailed. Geography, too, seems to play a part in determining collectibility. California dealer Judy Heidemann found that her customers preferred birdhouses with a traditional, countrified feeling—barns, cottages, peaked-roof bungalows. She suspects this represents a reaction to the predominant "cookie-cutter, tract-style" architecture of the area.

House Hunting

If you're looking exclusively for old birdhouses, the best buys can still be found at flea markets and farm sales, though more and more of these "finds" are being snapped up by dealers, often to be sold at many times their original prices. If you're determined to bypass the dealers, stick to rural areas of the United States, particularly in the South, Midwest, and New England, where most of the birdhouses were originally made and used. On the other hand, a reputable dealer—someone you know and trust—can steer you away from

A Biedermeier-style birdhouse would surely please discerning songbirds, but seems most comfortable in an elegant interior.

slick reproductions, and will often help you to locate specific styles and vintages.

Most older birdhouses on the market date from this century, though a few late-nineteenth-century models can still be found. Because they were usually crafted of perishable materials, and were used almost exclusively out-of-doors, birdhouses tended to succumb to the ravages of time and the weather (not to mention the birds and occasional rodents who made them their home). The majority of birdhouses that *did* manage to survive date from about 1910 through the 1940s.

Dating a birdhouse is no easy task, even for professionals. Prevailing architectural styles often offer a clue, though Victorian birdhouses, for example, have been popular from the 1900s to the present day. Embellishments can also help, especially datable ornaments like bottle caps and buttons. More important than pinning down an exact date is determining whether the birdhouse is genuinely old or a clever reproduction.

Because contemporary designers often use old barn wood in their birdhouses, Aarne Anton of New York's American Primitive Gallery always looks at the *edges* of the wood: newly cut edges will reveal tool marks and burrs. In many cases, these edges will be hidden or hand-softened to look old; if so, Anton advises, look at the entrance hole. Rain, sun, and the comings and goings of generations of birds tend to soften the edges of the entryway, and pecking and gnawing (by squatter rodents) often change its shape.

If the house is painted, look for a *gradation* in the weathering; the paint should be darkest under the eaves. Because they were frequently repainted, older houses tend to show layers of paint, often in a variety of colors. Hardware, too, can help unmask a pretender:

Folksy, funky, or elegantly architectural, birdhouses add visual interest to every conceivable interior style and can act as one-of-a-kind focal points.

look not just for rusted nails and screws (which can be easily faked) but vintage hardware *styles* (your local library can help here). And because older birdhouses were repaired from one season to the next, expect to find several *different* styles of hardware.

Finally, look for signs of use. Many older birdhouses still contain nests (sometimes layers of nests, if the houses couldn't be opened for cleaning). Bits of straw wedged into the woodwork and calcified droppings also indicate avian habitation. Beware the "antique" birdhouse with a spic-and-span interior.

Inside or Out?

Birdhouses were clearly designed for outdoor use, but not all can tolerate the out-of-doors. Most older birdhouses have endured decades of exposure to the elements; give them much more, and they're in danger of crumbling to dust. Even new birdhouses aren't necessarily weatherproof. Clifton Monteith's elegant and delicate bent-willow creations, for example, usually perch atop coffee tables and armoires; after years of outdoor use, he says, the natural-wood houses will begin to deteriorate. Find out from the manufacturer or craftsperson whether the house can tolerate outdoor exposure. If your interest in a birdhouse, old or new, is purely aesthetic—and if you've paid dearly for it—keep it inside. Hundreds of attractive contemporary birdhouses are designed to withstand the ravages of wind, sun, rain, and birds; stick to these if you're looking for a working birdhouse or garden ornament.

Nevertheless, some brave collectors insist on using their bird-

The sparse furnishings in this tower bedchamber highlight the room's spectacular proportions. A slender white birdhouse in the form of a country church enhances the serenity of the space and draws the eye to the elevated ceiling.

houses in the element for which they were designed. Alice Hoffman decorates her country house, inside *and* out, with the birdhouses she has collected over the years. She loves to cluster them in her garden, among the brilliance of summer flowers, and she keeps an oversized martin house on her back steps, where it can be easily admired from a living room window. Still, the rarest— and most expensive—houses in Hoffman's collection are snugly sheltered indoors.

One way to safely display a delicate birdhouse out-of-doors is to use it on a covered porch or in a screened sunroom. Susie Fisk-Stern shows off a tumbledown lighthouse/birdhouse on her Victorian porch; protected from the weather, it nevertheless seems very much in its element. On an eighteenth-century porch in Chesapeake, Virginia, a pillared birdhouse atop a nineteenth-century work table is part of a rural tableau, along with a chopping-block-turned-plant-stand, an antique dough-bowl, and an old wooden rake. The verandah of an Oregon farmhouse is decorated with flowers, quilts, and twig furniture; an old log birdhouse rests on a twig table alongside the nests that once decorated its interior. (Take note, however, that all birds, as well as their eggs and nests, are protected by the federal government; never remove a nest from the wild, and don't remove one from a birdhouse until you're sure the birds have left for the season.)

Porch and patio birdhouses need not be rustic to look at home in the out-of-doors. Against the porch wall of a whitewashed Colonial is a white church-style birdhouse from Lady Slipper Designs; it looks for all the world as if it were built into the original clapboard. And southwestern-style birdhouses of tin and painted wood adorn the adobe walls of many an enclosed Arizona patio.

Folk-art birdhouses have a natural affinity for country furnishings, as in this pine-paneled New England sitting room.

Decorating with Birdhouses

Part of the decorative appeal of birdhouses is their easy evocation of the out-of-doors. Hanging against lattice in a garden room or grouped with potted blooms on a wirework planter, birdhouses effectively bring an element of the outdoors to spaces that might otherwise seem enclosed. In the whimsically decorated potting shed of *Country Living* editor Niña Williams, a quintet of old birdhouses mingle on the open shelves of a painted armoire with terra-cotta pots, well-used gardening implements, and the muted pastels of dried flowers and herbs.

Of course, birdhouses make an eye-catching display in virtually any room of the house, equally at home on coffee tables, bedstands, and kitchen cabinets. In the dining room, a single architectural birdhouse, grouped with pots of flowering bulbs, makes a wonderful centerpiece for a Sunday brunch. Julie Stapleton, an Oregon antiques dealer, decorator, and birdhouse collector, groups birdhouses, nests, and sculptural moss-entwined branches for an outdoor effect in a corner of her dining room. (She sells her own painted birdhouses at her Estacada shop, the Tole Barn.)

Birdhouses have an affinity for natural materials; in a California beach house, a small blue-painted birdhouse is the stand-out element in a striking arrangement of driftwood, dried mesquite, and tumbleweed. And against the exposed-brick walls of the New York City floral shop VSF, a lean-to birdhouse looks right at home among dried hydrangeas, rosebuds, and gleaming pomegranates.

A single birdhouse—especially an elaborate or oversize model—can easily become the centerpiece of a room. But as any collector can attest, it's virtually impossible to resist the urge to add another—and another. Like the birds they were meant to shelter, birdhouses just seem to want to flock together.

BIRDHOUSE
PLANS

	A Size of Floor (inches/cm)	B Depth of Box (inches/cm)	C Height of Entrance above Floor (inches/cm)	D Diameter of Entrance Hole (inches/cm)	E Height above Ground (feet/meters)
Bluebird	5 x 5 (12.7 cm x 12.7 cm)	8 (20.3 cm)	6 (15.2 cm)	1 ½ (3.8 cm)	5–10 (1.5–3 m)
Chickadee	4 x 4 (10.2 cm x 10.2 cm)	8–10 (20.3–25.4 cm)	6–8 (15.2–20.3 cm)	1 ⅛ (2.9 cm)	6–15 (1.8–4.6 m)
Titmouse	4 x 4 (10.2 cm x 10.2 cm)	8–10 (20.3–25.4 cm)	6–8 (15.2–20.3 cm)	1 ¼ (3.2 cm)	6–15 (1.8–4.6 m)
Nuthatch	4 x 4 (10.2 cm x 10.2 cm)	8–10 (20.3–25.4 cm)	6–8 (15.2–20.3 cm)	1 ¼ (3.2 cm)	2–20 (.6–6.1 m)
House Wren and Bewick's Wren	4 x 4 (10.2 cm x 10.2 cm)	6–8 (15.2–20.3 cm)	4–6 (10.2–15.2 cm)	1–1 ¼ (2.5–3.2 cm)	6–10 (1.8–3 m)
Carolina Wren	4 x 4 (10.2 cm x 10.2 cm)	6–8 (15.2–20.3 cm)	4–6 (10.2–15.2 cm)	1 ½ (2.5–3.2 cm)	6–10 (1.8–3 m)
Violet-green Swallow and Tree Swallow	5 x 5 (12.7 cm x 12.7 cm)	6 (15.2 cm)	1–5 (2.5–12.7 cm)	1 ½ (3.8 cm)	10–15 (3–4.6 m)
Purple Martin	6 x 6 (15.2 cm x 15.2 cm)	6 (15.2 cm)	1 (2.5 cm)	2 ½ (6.4 cm)	15–20 (4.6–6.1 m)
House Finch	6 x 6 (15.2 cm x 15.2 cm)	6 (15.2 cm)	4 (10.2 cm)	2 (5.1 cm)	8–12 (2.4–3.7 m)
Starling	6 x 6 (15.2 cm x 15.2 cm)	16–18 (40.6–45.7 cm)	14–16 (35.6–40.6 cm)	2 (5.1 cm)	10–25 (3–7.6 m)
Crested Flycatcher	6 x 6 (15.2 cm x 15.2 cm)	8–10 (20.3–25.4 cm)	6–8 (15.2–20.3 cm)	2 (5.1 cm)	8–20 (2.4–6.1 m)
Flicker	7 x 7 (17.7 x 17.8 cm)	16–18 (40.6–45.7 cm)	14–16 (35.6–40.6 cm)	2 ½ (6.4 cm)	6–20 (1.8–6.1 m)
Golden-fronted Woodpecker and Red-headed Woodpecker	6 x 6 (15.2 cm x 15.2 cm)	12–15 (30.5–38.1 cm)	9–12 (22.9–30.5 cm)	2 (5.1 cm)	12–20 (3.7–6.1 m)
Downy Woodpecker	4 x 4 (10.2 cm x 10.2 cm)	8–10 (20.3–25.4 cm)	6–8 (15.2–20.3 cm)	1 ¼ (3.2 cm)	6–20 (1.8–6.1 m)
Hairy Woodpecker	6 x 6 (15.2 cm x 15.2 cm)	12–15 (30.5–38.1 cm)	9–12 (22.9–30.5 cm)	1 ½ (3.8 cm)	12–20 (3.7–6.1 m)
Screech Owl	8 x 8 (20.3 cm x 20.3 cm)	12–15 (30.5–38.1 cm)	9–12 (22.9–30.5 cm)	3 (7.6 cm)	10–30 (3–9.1 m)
Saw-whet Owl	6 x 6 (15.2 cm x 15.2 cm)	10–12 (25.4–30.5 cm)	8–10 (20.3–25.4 cm)	2 ½ (6.4 cm)	12–20 (3.7–6.1 m)
Barn Owl	10 x 18 (25.4 cm x 45.7 cm)	15–18 (38.1–45.7 cm)	4 (10.2 cm)	6 (15.2 cm)	12–18 (3.7–5.5 m)
American Kestrel	8 x 8 (20.3 cm x 20.3 cm)	12–15 (30.5–38.1 cm)	9–12 (22.9–30.5 cm)	3 (7.6 cm)	10–30 (3–9.1 m)
Wood Duck	10 x 18 (25.4 cm x 45.7 cm)	10–24 (25.4–61 cm)	12–16 (30.5–40.6 cm)	4 (10.2 cm)	10–20 (3–6.1 m)

Entrance Hole Sizes for Songbird, Woodpecker, and Squirrel Nest Box

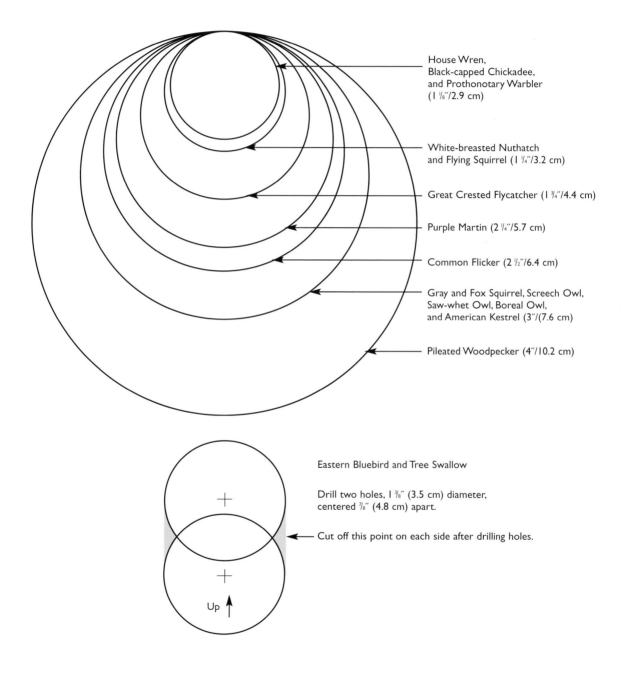

House Wren,
Black-capped Chickadee,
and Prothonotary Warbler
(1 ⅛″/2.9 cm)

White-breasted Nuthatch
and Flying Squirrel (1 ¼″/3.2 cm)

Great Crested Flycatcher (1 ¾″/4.4 cm)

Purple Martin (2 ¼″/5.7 cm)

Common Flicker (2 ½″/6.4 cm)

Gray and Fox Squirrel, Screech Owl,
Saw-whet Owl, Boreal Owl,
and American Kestrel (3″/7.6 cm)

Pileated Woodpecker (4″/10.2 cm)

Eastern Bluebird and Tree Swallow

Drill two holes, 1 ⅜″ (3.5 cm) diameter,
centered ⅞″ (4.8 cm) apart.

Cut off this point on each side after drilling holes.

Up ↑

SIMPLE
NEST BOXES

Songbird Box

(flycatchers, swallows, titmice, chickadees, nuthatches, wrens, and bluebirds)

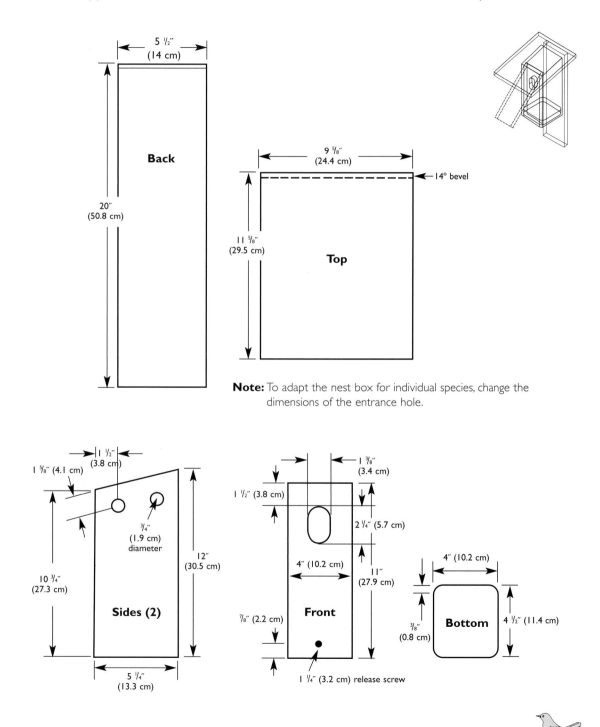

Back

5 ½″
(14 cm)

20″
(50.8 cm)

Top

9 ⅝″
(24.4 cm)

← 14° bevel

11 ⅝″
(29.5 cm)

Note: To adapt the nest box for individual species, change the dimensions of the entrance hole.

Sides (2)

1 ½″
(3.8 cm)

1 ⅝″ (4.1 cm)

¾″
(1.9 cm)
diameter

12″
(30.5 cm)

10 ¾″
(27.3 cm)

5 ¼″
(13.3 cm)

Front

1 ⅜″
(3.4 cm)

1 ½″ (3.8 cm)

2 ¼″ (5.7 cm)

4″ (10.2 cm)

11″
(27.9 cm)

⅞″ (2.2 cm)

1 ¼″ (3.2 cm) release screw

Bottom

4″ (10.2 cm)

⅜″
(0.8 cm)

4 ½″ (11.4 cm)

Purple Martin Gourd Condominium

1. Drill a 2″ (5.1 cm) diameter hole in the side of the gourd. This is the entryway for the birds.

2. Remove seeds and fibers from interior of gourd. Drill two holes in the upper neck of the gourd; these are used for attaching the gourd to the crosspiece.

3. If you wish for the gourds to last longer than a single season, give them two coats of polyurethane. This will prolong their life to two years.

4. Nail crosspieces to martin pole where desired. Wire or nail gourds to crosspieces at evenly spaced intervals. Erect martin pole by sinking it several feet into the ground to ensure its stability.

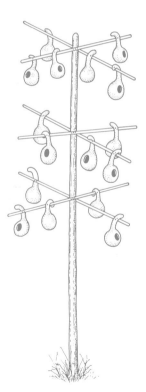

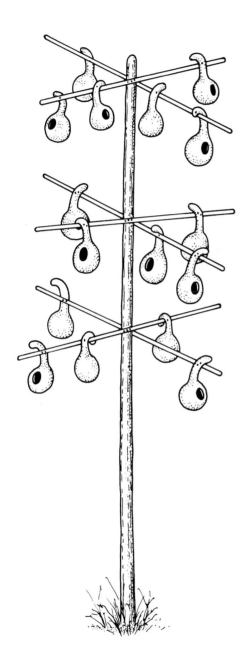

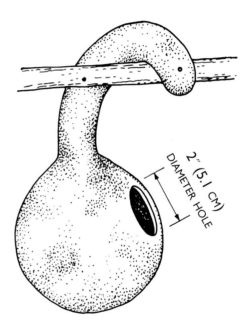

2" (5.1 CM) DIAMETER HOLE

Wren House

(house wren, black-capped chickadee, white-breasted nuthatch)

MATERIALS

1″ (2.5 cm)-thick cedar, pine, or fir, cut to the following dimensions:

two 6″ x 9″ (15.2 x 22.9 cm) boards (1A and 1B)

one 6 ½″ x 6 ¼″ (16.2 x 15.8 cm) board (2)

two 4″ x 7 ⅝″ (10.2 x 19.4 cm) boards (3A and 3B)

two 5″ x 7″ (12.7 x 17.7 cm) boards (4A and 4B)

two ¾″ x 4″ (1.9 x 10.2 cm) cleats

1. Bevel one 4″ (10.2 cm) edge of sides 3A and 3B at a 26° angle, and one 7″ (17.7 cm) edge of sides 4A and 4B at a 30° angle. Then, cut the top edges of sides 1A and 1B at a 30° angle to the horizontal. These will serve as the front and back of the birdhouse.

2. Make the entry hole for the front (side 1A) by drilling a circle at least 1 ⅛″ (2.9 cm) in diameter, but not much larger. This hole should be about 3″ (7.6 cm) from the top peak. Drill five evenly spaced ¼″ (0.6 cm)-diameter vent holes along the top edges of side 1B.

3. Attach the cleats to the base (side 2) as illustrated, sides 3A and 3B at their beveled end to the cleats, and sides 1A and 1B to the ends of the cleats. The top and sides 4A and 4B should be attached last, with their beveled edges fitting snugly together.

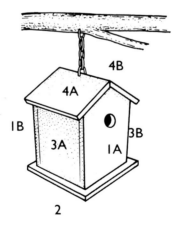

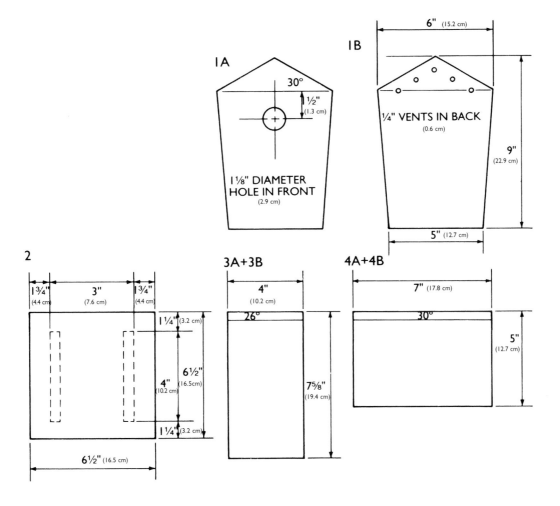

IA

30°

$1\frac{1}{2}$"
(1.3 cm)

$1\frac{1}{8}$" DIAMETER
HOLE IN FRONT
(2.9 cm)

IB

6" (15.2 cm)

$\frac{1}{4}$" VENTS IN BACK
(0.6 cm)

9"
(22.9 cm)

5" (12.7 cm)

2

$1\frac{3}{4}$"
(4.4 cm)

3"
(7.6 cm)

$\frac{3}{4}$"
(4.4 cm)

$1\frac{1}{4}$" (3.2 cm)

4"
(10.2 cm)

$6\frac{1}{2}$"
(16.5cm)

$1\frac{1}{4}$" (3.2 cm)

$6\frac{1}{2}$" (16.5 cm)

3A+3B

4"
(10.2 cm)

26°

$7\frac{5}{8}$"
(19.4 cm)

4A+4B

7" (17.8 cm)

30°

5"
(12.7 cm)

Northern Flicker Box

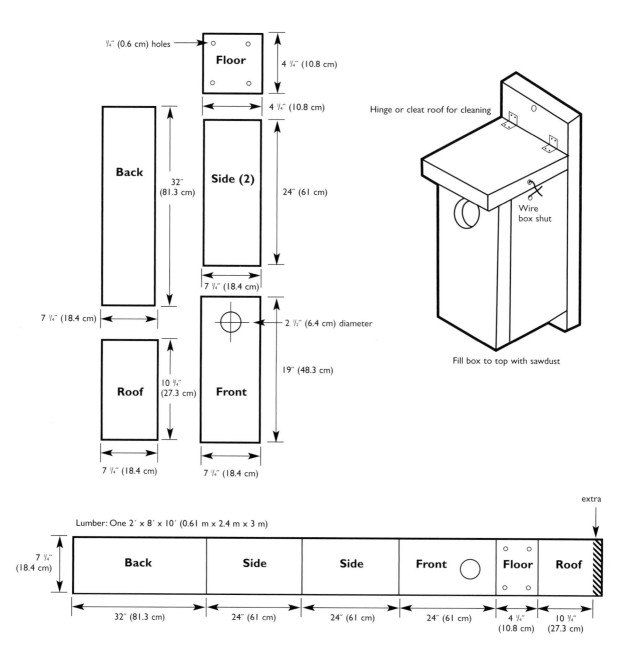

¼" (0.6 cm) holes

Floor

4 ¼" (10.8 cm)

4 ¼" (10.8 cm)

Back

32"
(81.3 cm)

Side (2)

24" (61 cm)

7 ¼" (18.4 cm)

7 ¼" (18.4 cm)

Hinge or cleat roof for cleaning

Wire
box shut

Roof

10 ¾"
(27.3 cm)

Front

2 ½" (6.4 cm) diameter

19" (48.3 cm)

Fill box to top with sawdust

7 ¼" (18.4 cm)

7 ¼" (18.4 cm)

extra

Lumber: One 2′ x 8′ x 10′ (0.61 m x 2.4 m x 3 m)

7 ¼"
(18.4 cm)

| **Back** | **Side** | **Side** | **Front** | **Floor** | **Roof** |

32" (81.3 cm) 24" (61 cm) 24" (61 cm) 24" (61 cm) 4 ¼" (10.8 cm) 10 ¾" (27.3 cm)

The New Birdhouse Book

Kestrel and Screech Owl Box

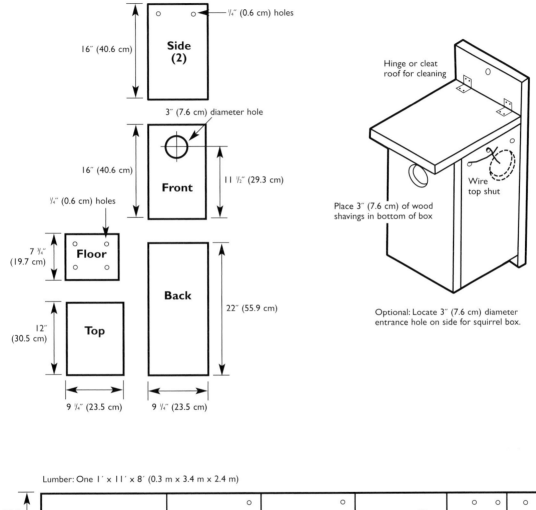

¼" (0.6 cm) holes

Side (2)

16" (40.6 cm)

3" (7.6 cm) diameter hole

16" (40.6 cm)

Front

11 ½" (29.3 cm)

¼" (0.6 cm) holes

7 ¾" (19.7 cm)

Floor

Back

22" (55.9 cm)

12" (30.5 cm)

Top

9 ¼" (23.5 cm)

9 ¼" (23.5 cm)

Hinge or cleat roof for cleaning

Wire top shut

Place 3" (7.6 cm) of wood shavings in bottom of box

Optional: Locate 3" (7.6 cm) diameter entrance hole on side for squirrel box.

Extra

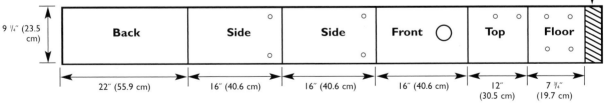

Lumber: One 1' x 11' x 8' (0.3 m x 3.4 m x 2.4 m)

9 ¼" (23.5 cm)

Back	**Side**	**Side**	**Front**	**Top**	**Floor**

22" (55.9 cm) 16" (40.6 cm) 16" (40.6 cm) 16" (40.6 cm) 12" (30.5 cm) 7 ¾" (19.7 cm)

Bluebird House

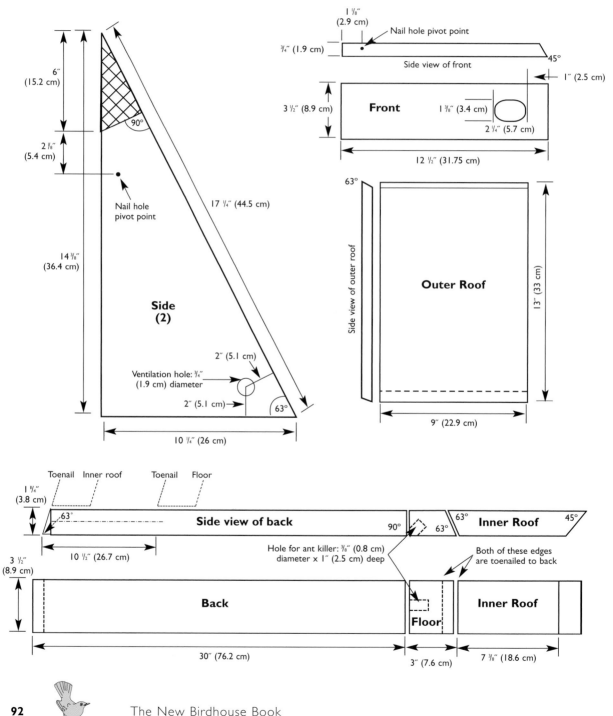

6″ (15.2 cm)

2 ⅛″ (5.4 cm)

Nail hole pivot point

17 ¼″ (44.5 cm)

14 ⅜″ (36.4 cm)

Side (2)

Ventilation hole: ¾″ (1.9 cm) diameter

2″ (5.1 cm)

2″ (5.1 cm)

90°

63°

10 ¼″ (26 cm)

1 ⅛″ (2.9 cm)

Nail hole pivot point

¾″ (1.9 cm)

Side view of front

45°

1″ (2.5 cm)

3 ½″ (8.9 cm)

Front

1 ⅜″ (3.4 cm)

2 ¼″ (5.7 cm)

12 ½″ (31.75 cm)

63°

Side view of outer roof

Outer Roof

13″ (33 cm)

9″ (22.9 cm)

Toenail   Inner roof   Toenail   Floor

1 ¼″ (3.8 cm)

63°

Side view of back

90°

63°

63°

Inner Roof

45°

10 ½″ (26.7 cm)

Hole for ant killer: ⅜″ (0.8 cm) diameter x 1″ (2.5 cm) deep

Both of these edges are toenailed to back

3 ½″ (8.9 cm)

Back

Floor

Inner Roof

30″ (76.2 cm)

3″ (7.6 cm)

7 ⅜″ (18.6 cm)

Robin and Barn Swallow Box

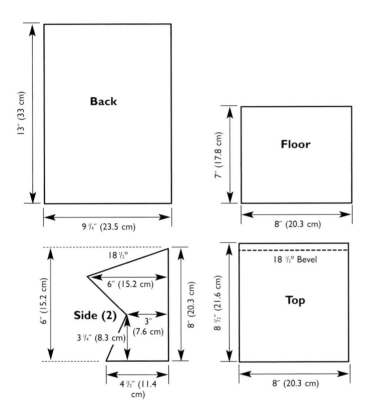

Back

13" (33 cm)

9 ¼" (23.5 cm)

Floor

7" (17.8 cm)

8" (20.3 cm)

18 ½°

6" (15.2 cm)

Side (2)

6" (15.2 cm)

3 ¼" (8.3 cm)

3" (7.6 cm)

8" (20.3 cm)

4 ½" (11.4 cm)

18 ½° Bevel

Top

8 ½" (21.6 cm)

8" (20.3 cm)

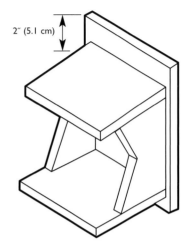

2" (5.1 cm)

Lumber: One 1" x 10" x 4' (2.5 cm x 25.4 cm x 1.2 m)

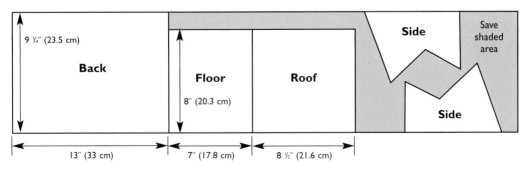

9 ¼" (23.5 cm)

Back

Floor

8" (20.3 cm)

Roof

Side

Save shaded area

Side

13" (33 cm)

7" (17.8 cm)

8 ½" (21.6 cm)

Gray Squirrel, Red Squirrel, and Fox Squirrel Box

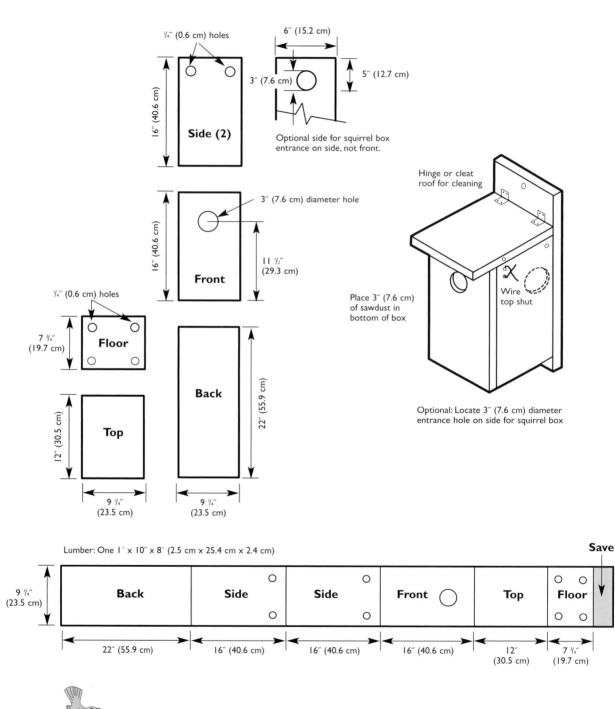

¼" (0.6 cm) holes

Side (2)

16" (40.6 cm)

6" (15.2 cm)

3" (7.6 cm)

5" (12.7 cm)

Optional side for squirrel box entrance on side, not front.

3" (7.6 cm) diameter hole

Front

16" (40.6 cm)

11 ½" (29.3 cm)

¼" (0.6 cm) holes

Floor

7 ¾" (19.7 cm)

Top

12" (30.5 cm)

Back

22" (55.9 cm)

9 ¼" (23.5 cm)

9 ¼" (23.5 cm)

Hinge or cleat roof for cleaning

Wire top shut

Place 3" (7.6 cm) of sawdust in bottom of box

Optional: Locate 3" (7.6 cm) diameter entrance hole on side for squirrel box

Lumber: One 1' x 10" x 8' (2.5 cm x 25.4 cm x 2.4 cm)

Save

9 ¼" (23.5 cm)

Back	Side	Side	Front	Top	Floor

22" (55.9 cm) | 16" (40.6 cm) | 16" (40.6 cm) | 16" (40.6 cm) | 12" (30.5 cm) | 7 ¾" (19.7 cm)

The New Birdhouse Book

Merganser and Wood Duck Box

Entrance Holes: Common Merganser—minimum 5″ (12.7 cm) diameter round

Wood Duck and Hooded Merganser—3″ (7.6 cm)-high × 4″ (10.2 cm)-wide oval

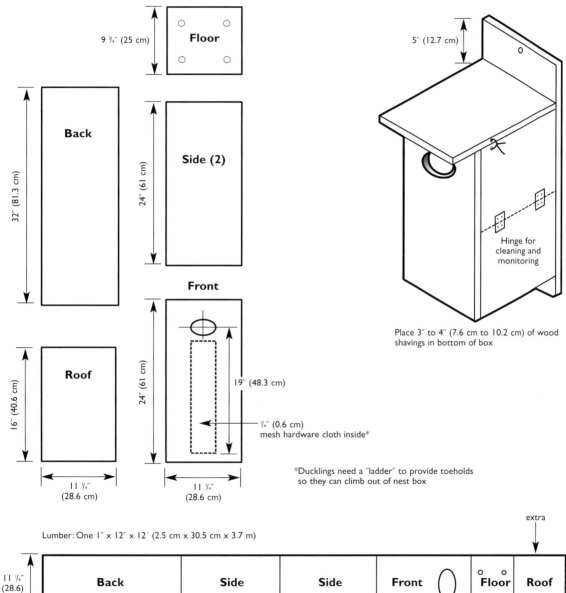

9 ¾″ (25 cm)

Floor

Back

32″ (81.3 cm)

Side (2)

24″ (61 cm)

Front

24″ (61 cm)

19″ (48.3 cm)

¼″ (0.6 cm)
mesh hardware cloth inside*

Roof

16″ (40.6 cm)

11 ¼″
(28.6 cm)

11 ¼″
(28.6 cm)

5″ (12.7 cm)

Hinge for
cleaning and
monitoring

Place 3″ to 4″ (7.6 cm to 10.2 cm) of wood
shavings in bottom of box

*Ducklings need a "ladder" to provide toeholds
so they can climb out of nest box

Lumber: One 1″ x 12″ x 12′ (2.5 cm x 30.5 cm x 3.7 m)

extra

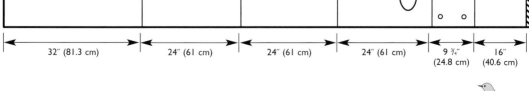

11 ¼″
(28.6)

Back	**Side**	**Side**	**Front**	**Floor**	**Roof**

32″ (81.3 cm)　　24″ (61 cm)　　24″ (61 cm)　　24″ (61 cm)　　9 ¾″ (24.8 cm)　　16″ (40.6 cm)

Great Blue Heron Nest Platform

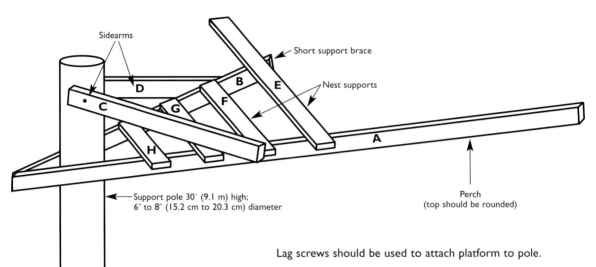

Sidearms

Short support brace

Nest supports

D

B

E

C

G

F

H

A

Support pole 30′ (9.1 m) high;
6″ to 8″ (15.2 cm to 20.3 cm) diameter

Perch
(top should be rounded)

Lag screws should be used to attach platform to pole.

Position sidearms on support pole so nest is inclined upward at approximately 7° angle.

Wire armful of sticks on lath nest supports to stimulate use.

LUMBER:

A. 2″ x 2″ x 7′ (5.1 cm x 5.1 cm x 2.1 m)

B. 2″ x 2″ x 30″(5.1 cm x 5.1 cm x 76.2 cm)

C. 1″ x 2″ x 26 ½″ (2.5 cm x 5.1 cm x 67.3 cm)

D. 1″ x 2″ x 26 ½″ (2.5 cm x 5.1 cm x 67.3 cm)

E. 1″ x 2″ x 39″ (2.5 cm x 5.1 cm x 99.1 cm)

F. 1″ x 2″ x 19 ½″ (2.5 cm x 5.1 cm x 49.5 cm)

G. 1″ x 2″ x 19 ¼″ (2.5 cm x 5.1 cm x 48.9 cm)

H. 1″ x 2″ x 17 ⅞″ (2.5 cm x 5.1 cm x 45.4 cm)

One 30′ (9.1 m) cedar support pole/three platforms, staggered at 180° and 4′ (1.2 m) intervals

The New Birdhouse Book

Tree Swallow Box

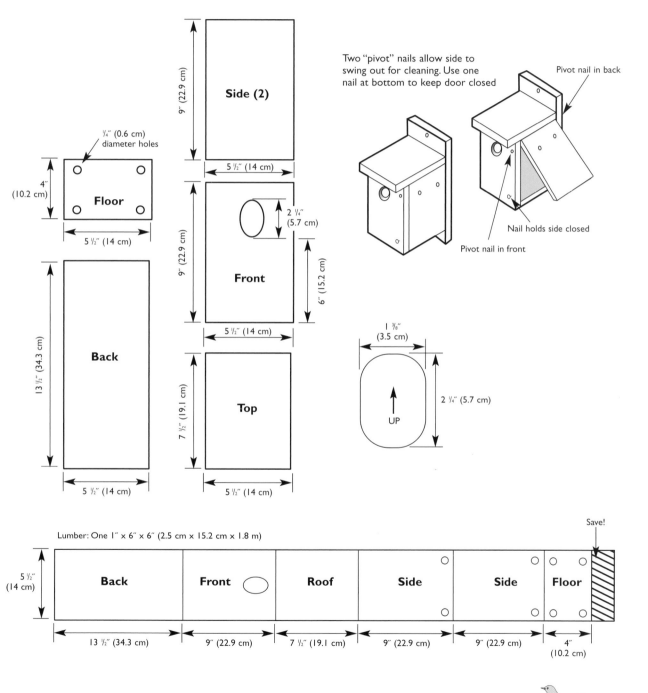

¼" (0.6 cm) diameter holes

Floor

4" (10.2 cm)

5 ½" (14 cm)

Side (2)

9" (22.9 cm)

5 ½" (14 cm)

Front

9" (22.9 cm)

5 ½" (14 cm)

2 ¼" (5.7 cm)

6" (15.2 cm)

Back

13 ½" (34.3 cm)

5 ½" (14 cm)

Top

7 ½" (19.1 cm)

5 ½" (14 cm)

Two "pivot" nails allow side to swing out for cleaning. Use one nail at bottom to keep door closed

Pivot nail in back

Nail holds side closed

Pivot nail in front

1 ⅜" (3.5 cm)

2 ¼" (5.7 cm)

UP

Lumber: One 1" x 6" x 6" (2.5 cm x 15.2 cm x 1.8 m)

Save!

5 ½" (14 cm)

Back	**Front**	**Roof**	**Side**	**Side**	**Floor**
13 ½" (34.3 cm)	9" (22.9 cm)	7 ½" (19.1 cm)	9" (22.9 cm)	9" (22.9 cm)	4" (10.2 cm)

Hollow Log Box

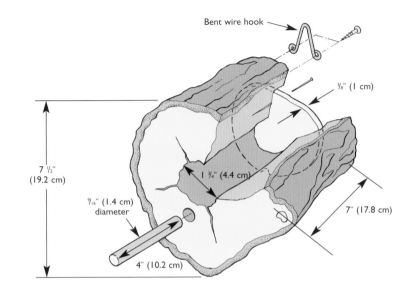

MATERIALS

I short log 8″ –14″
(20.3 cm–35.6 cm) diameter

I piece of 6″ × 6″ × ⅜″
or ¼″ (15.2 cm × 15.2
× I cm or 0.6 cm) plywood

I piece of 3″ × ¼″
(7.6 cm × 0.6 cm) diameter dowel

I length of stiff wire

screws

OTHER TOOLS

Router and large diameter
(¾″ (1.9 cm) plus) straight bit

½″ (1.3 cm) diameter flat
or spade bit

CUTTING THE HOLE

I. Cut both faces of the branch or log with a saw, leaving it flat and reasonably smooth. If required, use a chisel and wooden mallet to enlarge the hole. Work with the grain direction, cutting away thin shavings. If you wish to cut a new hole in a log, use a flat bit or auger to drill a ring of holes. Knock out the center waste and pare the sides with a chisel to finish them smooth.

2. Choose a round container, paint can or similar, that is about I″ (2.5 cm) larger in diameter than the irregular hole in the log. Place this over the irregular hole and draw round it with a pencil.

3. Fit a large-diameter straight cutter in the electric router.

4. Set the depth of cut to ⅛″ (0.3 cm). With the router firmly supported on the timber face and firmly gripped in both hands, cut round the edge of the hole in a clockwise direction. Aim to remove

about ¼″ (0.6 cm) of wood from the edge at a time, slowly increasing the rebated area up to the line. Having cut around the line, increase the depth of cut and repeat the process until the full ½″ (1.3 cm) is completely removed.

5. Alternatively, a sharp chisel can be used, first marking the depth of the hole and cutting from the side before cutting to clear the remaining wood. Use a wooden mallet to drive the chisel.

END PLATES

6. On ⅜″ (1 cm) plywood, draw around the container used to mark out the rebate. Cut out the circular plate with a jigsaw and trim with a rasp until it is a fairly close fit in the rebate in the log.

7. Use a holesaw to cut the entrance hole when fitting a plate to the front of a hollow log. Drill a small hole or cut a small notch at the bottom of the plate to allow for drainage.

8. If preferred, the outside face of the plate can be painted with masonry paint or water-based stain or varnish, before being fitted.

9. Screw or nail the plate into the rebate.

MOUNTING

10. To enable the log to be hung on a wall or post, bend a piece of stiff wire with a circular twist at each end, and fix it to the back of the log with two wood screws.

The New Birdhouse Book

Clay Pot Boxes

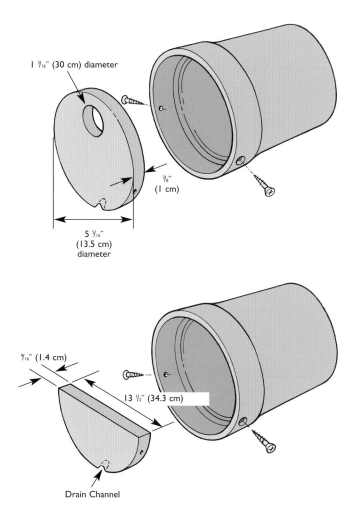

1 ¹¹/₁₆″ (30 cm) diameter

³/₈″
(1 cm)

5 ⁵/₁₆″
(13.5 cm)
diameter

⁹/₁₆″ (1.4 cm)

13 ½″ (34.3 cm)

Drain Channel

MATERIALS

Terra-cotta flowerpots 6″–12″
(15.2 cm–30.5 cm) diameter

1 piece of 12″ × 12″ × ³/₈″ or ¼″
(30.5 cm × 30.5 cm × 1 cm or 0.6 cm)
plywood

Screws

Terra-cotta paint

1. Using any size of traditional terra-cotta flowerpot, measure the inside diameter within the stepped rim of the pot.

2. Set a pair of compasses to that diameter and draw out the circle on ³/₈″ (1 cm) thick solid wood or plywood. Score along the line and cut around it with a jigsaw.

3. Use a masonry bit to drill two holes in opposite sides of the pot rim, and use a larger drill to countersink them.

4. Either cut an entrance hole, the size depending on the pot and the bird species you wish to attract, or cut part of the circle away to produce an open-front birdhouse. At the bottom of the disk cut a small notch across its edge to allow the pot to drain if necessary.

5. Block the drainage hole in the base of the terra-cotta pot with an epoxy filler plug.

6. Fit the disk in the rim of the pot and insert the two screws.

7. Paint the outside face of the disk with terra-cotta masonry paint.

MOUNTING

8. Use stiff garden wire to make a cradle for hanging the pot in a tree or bush. Alternatively, cut a small-diameter wooden disk, slightly larger than the drainage hole in the end of the pot, and drill a hole through its center. Screw the pot onto a wall or wooden surface using a long wood screw and an angle block to tilt the pot downward.

A-Frame Bird Box

MATERIALS

1 piece of 24″ x 24″ x ⅜″
(61 cm x 61 cm x 1 cm)
plywood

1 piece of 3″ x ⅜″ diameter
(7.6 cm x 1 cm) dowel

1 piece of 6″ x 1″ x ⅜″
(15.2 cm x 2.5 cm x 1 cm)
timber

1 piece of 12″ x 3″ x ¾″
(30.5 cm x 7.6 cm x 1.3 cm)
timber

Exterior wood glue

Stain and paint

¾″ (1.3 cm) molding pins

Brass hook and eye

BACK AND ROOF

1. Cut the triangular (45°:45°:90°) back panel and two roof panels from ⅜″ (1 cm) plywood, scoring across the grain with a craft knife and finishing the edges square with a plane.

2. Plane a bevel of 45° along one short edge of the two roof panels.

3. Glue and pin the two roof panels to the triangular back, leaving a ¼″ (0.6 cm) lip along the rear edges.

FRONT

4. Cut the triangular and bottom panels from ⅜″ (1 cm) plywood and plane the edges square. Finish the length of the bottom panel the same dimension as the base of the triangular front. Trim both ends of the bottom to an angle of 45°. Glue and pin the two pieces together, with a ⅛″ (0.3 cm) overlap to leave a lip along the bottom edge.

5. Drill the entrance hole with a 1–1 ¼″ (2.5 cm–3.2 cm) diameter holesaw to suit the specific bird species. Cut a 3″ (7.6 cm) length of ¼″ (0.6 cm) diameter dowel and glue it into a hole drilled beneath the entrance hole.

6. After filling any defects and recessed pin and screw heads with epoxy filler, sand all surfaces smooth. Paint the outer walls, roof, and base with an exterior masonry paint or water-based stain or varnish.

SLIDES

7. Cut a solid batten (8 ¼″ x ¾″ x ¼″ (21 cm x 1.9 cm x 0.6 cm)) and plane a 45° angle along one edge. Cut the batten in half, and, with the front of the box in place, glue and pin each piece to the inside face of the roof panels, checking that the front slides in and out easily. Wipe away any excess glue before leaving to dry.

8. Fit a small brass hook to the bottom edge of the rear panel to locate into a brass eye screwed into the underside of the floor.

MOUNTING

9. Cut the rear mounting bracket and the spacing piece from a piece of 3″ x ¾″ (7.6 cm x 1.9 cm) wood and trim one end of both pieces to a 45° apex. Glue and screw the two pieces to the back panel, ensuring that the screws do not penetrate into the nesting box.

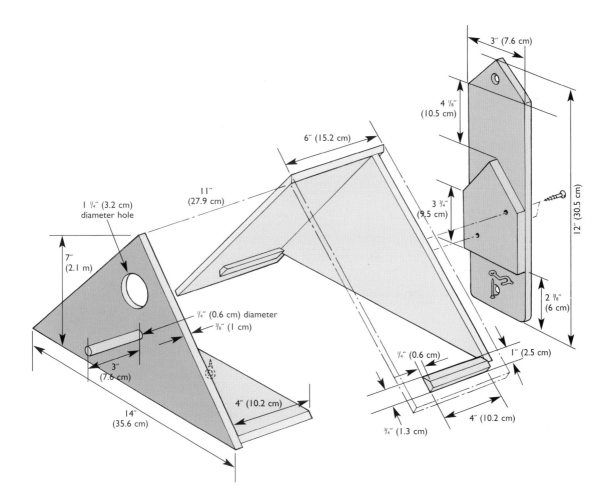

3″ (7.6 cm)

4 ⅛″
(10.5 cm)

6″ (15.2 cm)

11″
(27.9 cm)

1 ¼″ (3.2 cm)
diameter hole

3 ¾″
(9.5 cm)

12″ (30.5 cm)

7″
(2.1 m)

¼″ (0.6 cm) diameter
⅜″ (1 cm)

2 ⅜″
(6 cm)

3″
(7.6 cm)

4″ (10.2 cm)

¼″ (0.6 cm)

1″ (2.5 cm)

14″
(35.6 cm)

¾″ (1.3 cm)

4″ (10.2 cm)

Classic Bird Box

MATERIALS

1 piece of 30″ x 18″ x 3/8″ (76.2 cm x 45.7 cm x 1 cm) plywood

1 piece of 12″ x 3″ x 3/4″ (30.5 cm x 7.6 cm x 1.3 cm) timber

1 piece of 6″ x 1/2″ x 1/2″ (15.2 cm x 1.3 cm x 1.3 cm) triangular bead

Exterior wood glue

Stain and paint

3/4″ (1.9 cm) molding pins

1 brass hinge

WALLS

1. Cut four sides, one each 6″ x 7 3/4″ (15.2 cm x 19.7 cm) and 6″ x 9 3/4″ (15.2 cm x 24.8 cm) and two 5 1/2″ x 9 1/4″ (14 cm x 23.5 cm) from 3/8″ (1 cm) plywood.

2. Mark out the roof angle on two side pieces. Score across the grain and cut to this angle. Clamp both sides together in a vise and plane to the same size, leaving the edges square.

3. Mark out the rebate on the vertical inside face of the front and back. These are equal to the thickness of the plywood, 3/8″ (1 cm) on the inside face of each piece and to a depth of 3/16″ (0.5 cm).

4. Score across the grain on both pieces, before cutting with a backsaw to the depth on the inside of the line. Pare the plywood veneers away with a chisel to form the rebates.

5. Glue and pin the four walls together, checking that the bottom edges are flush and that the corners are square.

6. When dry, plane the top edge of the front and rear walls to follow the side-wall roof angle.

7. Cut the floor from 3/8″ (1 cm) plywood, to a push fit inside the walls. Plane the edges square and trim the corners at 45° (for drainage). Drill the four walls and screw the floor in place.

8. Draw a center line down the front face. Cut the entrance hole with a 1″–1 1/4″ (2.5 cm–3.2 cm) holesaw to suit specific species. Alternatively, cut a 1 1/2″ (3.8 cm) deep slot across the top of the front panel, finishing at each end in a curve.

9. Cut the 8 1/2″ x 8 1/2″ (21.6 cm x 21.6 cm) roof from 3/8″ (1 cm) plywood and plane the edges square.

10. Cut and miter four lengths of 1/2″ (1.3 cm) half-round bead and glue and pin them to the roof edges.

FINISHING TOUCHES

11. After filling any defects and recessed pin and screw heads with epoxy filler, sand all surfaces smooth. Paint the outer walls, roof, and base with nontoxic stain or varnish or masonry paint. After painting, screw the lid to the box using a 1 1/2″ (3.8 cm) brass hinge.

MOUNTING

12. From 3/4″ (1.9 cm) wood, cut a 3″ x 13 1/2″ (7.6 cm x 34.3 cm) plate and round each end. Drill and countersink two 3/16″ (0.5 cm) screw holes at each end. From 1 1/2″ (3.8 cm) lumber, cut a 3″ x 2 1/2″ (7.6 cm x 6.4 cm) block. Screw and glue the block to the back of the box and screw the plate to it.

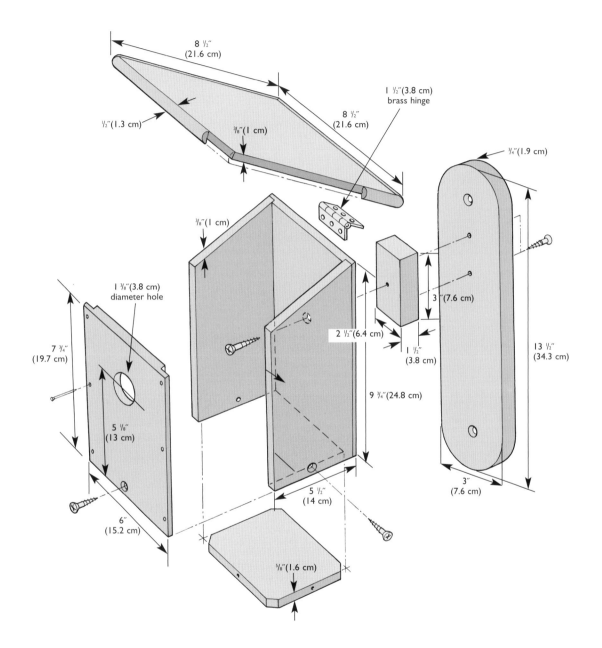

8 ½"
(21.6 cm)

1 ½"(3.8 cm)
brass hinge

8 ½"
(21.6 cm)

¾"(1.9 cm)

½"(1.3 cm)

⅜"(1 cm)

⅜"(1 cm)

1 ⅜"(3.8 cm)
diameter hole

2 ½"(6.4 cm)

3"(7.6 cm)

1 ½"
(3.8 cm)

13 ½"
(34.3 cm)

7 ¾"
(19.7 cm)

5 ⅛"
(13 cm)

9 ¾"(24.8 cm)

6"
(15.2 cm)

5 ½"
(14 cm)

3"
(7.6 cm)

⅝"(1.6 cm)

Wood Shed Box

MATERIALS

1 piece of 18″ x 18″ x ¼″
(45.7 cm x 45.7 cm x 0.6 cm) plywood

1 piece of 8″ x ¼″
(20.3 cm x 0.6 cm) diameter dowel

1 piece of 10″ x ¼″
(25.4 cm x 0.6 cm) timber

1 piece of 8″ x 6″ x ½″
(20.3 cm x 15.2 cm x 1.3 cm)
plywood

Exterior wood glue

Stain and paint

¾″ (1.9 cm) molding pins

WALLS

1. Cut two 4″ x 7 ¾″ (10.2 cm x 19.7 cm) and two 3 ½″ x 7 ¾″ (8.9 cm x 19.7 cm) pieces from ¼″ (0.6 cm) plywood. Clamp each pair in turn in a vise and plane to the same size, leaving the edges square.

2. Draw out on the larger two, the 45° roof pitch. Score across the grain and cut to this angle. Plane a 45° chamfer along the top edges of the smaller side walls.

3. Mark out the rebate on the vertical panels of the front and back. This is equal to the thickness of the plywood (¼″ (0.6 cm)) on the inside face of each piece and to the depth of three veneers (layers) on the edges.

4. Score across the grain on both pieces, before cutting with a backsaw to the depth of three veneers. Pare the veneers away with a chisel to form the rebates.

5. Carefully mark out the window and door openings, and score across the grain where necessary. Make the openings using a backsaw to cut down the grain and a coping saw to cut across. Finish the edges with a file and abrasive paper, leaving a straight edge.

6. Glue and pin the sides together and check that the corners are square. When dry, plane or sand the edges flush.

ROOF

7. Cut the roof panels to size and plane the edges square. Mark out and cut the 45° triangular end pieces to size and plane the edges square. Glue and pin the panels together to form the pitched roof. Cut a ¼″ (0.6 cm) diameter length of dowel 2″ (5.1 cm) longer than the roof, and glue it in the 90° angle left along the apex of the roof.

BASE

8. Mark out the outside edges of the 8″ x 5 ¾″ (20.3 cm x 14.6 cm) base and the corner radius. Score across the grain and around the corner radius. Cut the base out with a jigsaw and finish by planning the straight edges and sanding the corners smooth with sanding block and abrasive paper.

9. Draw the cutout for the shed on the base and score across the grain. Cut the openings using a backsaw to cut down the grain and a coping saw to cut across. Fit the assembled walls into the cutout, gluing and pinning through the front and side walls.

WINDOWS AND DOOR

10. Cut the two window panels, sand smooth and paint black, leaving a glue margin on three sides. Glue the panels to the inside of the side walls and clamp until dry.

11. Cut out the door and floor of the nesting box, and cut the angled corners of the latter. Glue and pin the pieces together allowing adequate depth for the nest (this may vary with the species size), to prevent the young chicks from falling or climbing too easily through the entrance hole, until they are ready to leave the nest.

12. Cut the entrance hold with a holesaw of 1″–1 ¼″ (2.5 cm–3.2 cm) to suit specific bird species. Cut a 2″ (5.1 cm) length of ¼″ (0.6 cm) diameter dowel and glue it into a hole drilled beneath the entrance hole.

13. After filling any defects and recessed pin and screw heads with epoxy filler, sand all surfaces smooth. Paint the outer walls, roof, and base with a water-based stain or varnish.

SEAT PERCH

14. Draw out the two seat ends, but before scoring and cutting the ⅛″ (0.3 cm) thick plywood, cut the holes for the seat slats by first drilling a row of 3/32″ (0.2 cm) holes and then cutting out the waste with a fretsaw. Score across the grain and carefully cut out the seat ends with the fretsaw.

15. Cut three 2 ½″ x 3/32″ (6.4 cm x 0.2 cm) solid slats and glue them into the slots in the seat ends. Drill the baseboard to take four fine pins and glue and pin the seat to the base. To allow the glue to stick to the wood, scrape away an area of paint from the point where the seat legs touch the base. Finish the seat with either paint or varnish.

MOUNTING

16. The box can be hung on a wall by fitting a short batten to the rear of the box, or alternatively mount on a post of a similar section as the inside dimensions of the box.

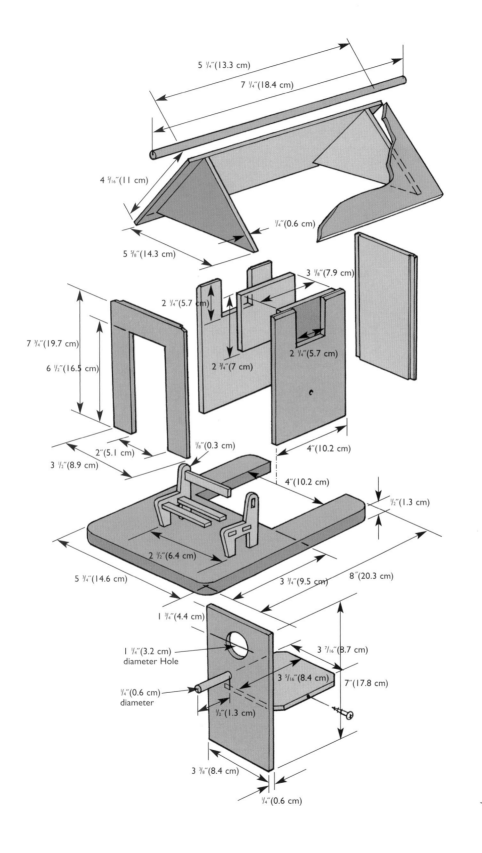

5 1/4"(13.3 cm)

7 1/4"(18.4 cm)

4 5/16"(11 cm)

1/4"(0.6 cm)

5 5/8"(14.3 cm)

3 1/8"(7.9 cm)

2 1/4"(5.7 cm)

2 3/4"(7 cm)

2 1/4"(5.7 cm)

7 3/4"(19.7 cm)

6 1/2"(16.5 cm)

4"(10.2 cm)

1/8"(0.3 cm)

2"(5.1 cm)

3 1/2"(8.9 cm)

4"(10.2 cm)

1/2"(1.3 cm)

2 1/2"(6.4 cm)

5 3/4"(14.6 cm)

3 3/4"(9.5 cm)

8"(20.3 cm)

1 3/4"(4.4 cm)

1 1/4"(3.2 cm)
diameter Hole

3 7/16"(8.7 cm)

1/4"(0.6 cm)
diameter

3 5/16"(8.4 cm)

7"(17.8 cm)

1/2"(1.3 cm)

3 3/8"(8.4 cm)

1/4"(0.6 cm)

105

Southwest Hacienda

MATERIALS

1 piece of 24″ x 24″ x ⅜″
(61 cm x 61 cm x 1 cm) plywood

1 piece of 48″ x 1″ (121.9 cm x 2.5
cm) half-round bead

Exterior wood glue

Screws

Stain and paint

¾″ (1.9 cm) molding pins

WALLS

1. Draw the front and back panels out on
⅜″ (1 cm) plywood, following the drawing. Score across the grain and cut on the
waste side of the line. Clamp both pieces
in a vise, and finish the edges straight and
square with a plane or file. Cut out the
arched door, windows and belfry and finish the cut edges with abrasive paper
wrapped over straight or rounded sanding block.

2. Cut the two side walls (4″ x 7 ⅛″ (10.2
cm x 18.1 cm)) and two roof sections (4″
x 5 ¾″ (10.2 cm x 14.6 cm)) from ⅜″ (1
cm) plywood. Plane the edges square and
plane a 45° bevel on one end of each. Cut
the small roof section (4″ x 2 ⅜″ (10.2 cm
x 5.9 cm)) and plane the edges square.

3. Glue and pin the side walls and roof
section between the front and back walls,
checking that all remains square.

4. Cut six 5″ (15.2 cm) length of ¾″ (1.9
cm) half-round bead and plane a narrow
flat along each edge. Glue and pin the
bead to the pitched roof.

NESTING BOX

5. Cut a rectangular piece of ⅜″ (1 cm)
plywood equal to the distance between
the side walls and ½″ (1.3 cm) higher than
the door opening. Set this in the opening
and draw in the opening's outline. Find
the center of the arch and use it as the
center point for the entrance hole. Drill
the hole using a 1″ (2.5 cm) holesaw.

6. Cut a rectangular piece of ⅜″ (1 cm)
plywood 4″ x 3 ⅞″ (10.2 cm x 9.8 cm),
and trim the corners at 45° (for
drainage). Screw and glue this to the
door panel 3″ (7.6 cm) below the
entrance hole. Depending on the bird
species you wish to attract, a ¼″ (0.6 cm)
diameter perch can be added. Alternatively, the door panel can be cut lower
to produce an open-fronted box. Drill
through the side wall to locate the nesting floor with a brass screw or loose pin.

FINISHING TOUCHES

7. After filling any defects and recessed
pin and screw heads with epoxy filler,
sand all surfaces smooth. Paint the outer
walls, roof, and base with nontoxic stain
or varnish or masonry paint. After painting, screw the lid to the box using a 1 ½″
(3.8 cm) brass hinge.

The New Birdhouse Book

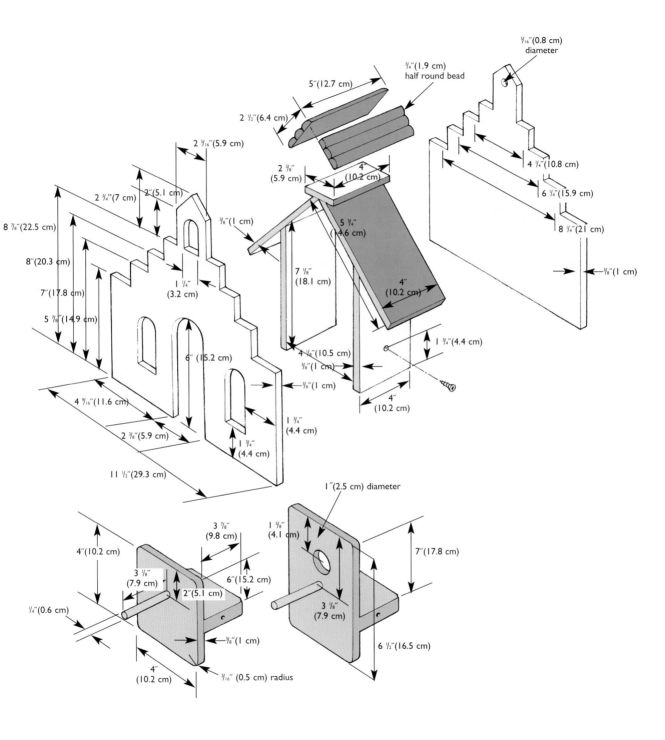

5⁄16″(0.8 cm) diameter

5″(12.7 cm)

¾″(1.9 cm) half round bead

2 ½″(6.4 cm)

2 5⁄16″(5.9 cm)

2 ¾″(7 cm)

2″(5.1 cm)

8 7⁄8″(22.5 cm)

8″(20.3 cm)

7″(17.8 cm)

5 7⁄8″(14.9 cm)

4 9⁄16″(11.6 cm)

2 3⁄8″(5.9 cm)

11 ½″(29.3 cm)

1 ¼″ (3.2 cm)

6″ (15.2 cm)

3⁄8″(1 cm)

1 ¾″ (4.4 cm)

2 3⁄8″ (5.9 cm)

4″ (10.2 cm)

4″ (10.2 cm)

5 ¾″ (14.6 cm)

4″ (10.2 cm)

7 1⁄8″ (18.1 cm)

4 1⁄8″(10.5 cm)

3⁄8″(1 cm)

3⁄8″(1 cm)

1 ¾″(4.4 cm)

4″ (10.2 cm)

4 ¼″(10.8 cm)

6 ¼″(15.9 cm)

8 ¼″(21 cm)

3⁄8″(1 cm)

1″(2.5 cm) diameter

1 5⁄8″ (4.1 cm)

7″(17.8 cm)

3 7⁄8″ (9.8 cm)

4″(10.2 cm)

3 1⁄8″ (7.9 cm)

2″(5.1 cm)

6″(15.2 cm)

¼″(0.6 cm)

3⁄8″(1 cm)

4″ (10.2 cm)

3⁄16″ (0.5 cm) radius

3 1⁄8″ (7.9 cm)

6 ½″(16.5 cm)

Prairie House

MATERIALS

2 pieces of 84″ × 1″
(213.4 cm × 2.5 cm) diameter dowel

1 piece 12″ × 3″ × ¾″
(25.4 cm × 7.6 cm × 1.9 cm) timber

1 piece of 14″ × 30″ × ½″ (35.6 cm ×
76.2 cm × 1.3 cm) plywood

1 piece of 9″ × 3″ × ¾″ (22.9 cm ×
7.6 cm × 1.9 cm) timber (blocks)

1 piece of 10 ¾″ × 3″ × 1″
(27.3 cm × 7.6 cm × 2.5 cm) timber

1 piece of 8″ × ⅜″ (20.3 cm × 1 cm)
quarter-round bead

1 piece of 18″ × 14″ × ½″ (45.7 cm ×
35.6 cm × 1.3 cm) plywood

1 piece of 13 ½″ × ¼″
(34.3 cm × 0.6 cm) diameter dowel

1 piece of 2″ × ½″
(5.1 cm × ⅓ cm) diameter dowel

Exterior wood glue

Stain and paint

¾″ (1.9 cm) molding pins

Screws

WALLS

1. The walls and roof of this log cabin are made from 1″ (2.5 cm) half-round bead. Alternatively, use 1″ (2.5 cm) dowel (or broom handle) sawn along its length.

2. Cut the two end panels from ¾″ (1 cm) plywood, scoring across the grain with a craft knife and finishing the edges square with a plane.

3. Drill the entrance hole with a holesaw to suit specific bird species.

4. Cut the half-round dowel into seven lengths and plane a narrow flat along each edge. This is to allow adequate edge width to form a horizontal glue joint between each piece. Cut one piece in half lengthwise for the top rails.

5. Glue and pin the rails to the two end pieces, gluing each horizontal joint as you proceed, and check that the end panels are vertical and square to the sides. Fit the narrow pieces at the top of the wall, and when dry, plane the top edges to follow the roof angle.

6. Cut the flat center roof-ridge member to length from ⅛″ (0.3 cm) plywood to finish flush with the outer face of the two end walls. Glue and pin this in place. When dry, plane the edges to match the roof angle.

7. Cut the two roof panels to size from ⅛″ (0.3 cm) plywood, again finishing flush with the outer face of the end and side walls. Glue and pin both panels in place.

8. Cut 22 lengths of half-round dowel ¼″ (0.6 cm) longer than the width of the angled roof panels. Glue and pin these to the roof panels, checking that no pins protrude through the underside. Arrange the pieces to leave equal overhang at either end and lay the top ends flush with top edges of the panels.

9. Carefully cut the top corner of each piece to form a flat surface on either side of the ridge board. Glue and pin a length of half-dowel flat onto the ridge board starting from the chimney end.

10. Cut the chimney from a 10 ¼″ (26 cm)-piece of 3″ × 1 ⅛″ (8.6 cm × 2.9 cm) wood, using a backsaw to cut partway down the length and across at an angle of 45° to form the narrow section. Cut two ⅛″ (0.3 cm) grooves at the top. Cut a ⅛″ (0.3 cm) plywood plate slightly larger than the chimney top and glue and pin it over the grooves. Glue and screw the chimney to the end wall.

11. Cut four short lengths of half-dowel to form the vertical corner pieces and further lengths to fit between these to cover the rear wall. Repeat this on the front wall, leaving the window and door openings.

NESTING COMPARTMENTS

12. Many smaller birds prefer a smaller nesting space. To encourage specific species, the inside of this box and the hole size can be adapted to suit. For larger species the nesting compartment can be omitted and the hole enlarged.

13. Cut the vertical division to fit to the underside of the roof. Cut the floor to the width of the house and glue and pin the two pieces together. Cut two 5″ (12.7 cm) pieces of ¾″ (1.9 cm) quarter-round bead, support battens slightly shorter than half the internal house length and glue them to the inside walls. Two small blocks prevent the nesting compartment from tipping back.

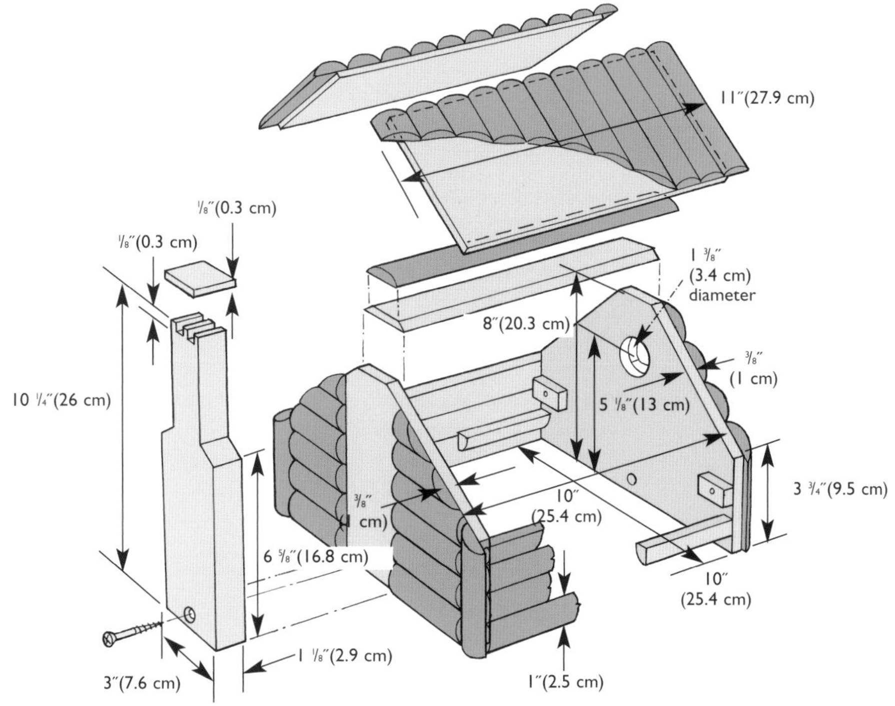
11″(27.9 cm)
1/8″(0.3 cm)
1/8″(0.3 cm)
1 3/8″
(3.4 cm)
diameter
8″(20.3 cm)
3/8″
(1 cm)
10 1/4″(26 cm)
5 1/8″(13 cm)
3 3/4″(9.5 cm)
3/8″
(1 cm)
10″
(25.4 cm)
6 5/8″(16.8 cm)
10″
(25.4 cm)
1 1/8″(2.9 cm)
3″(7.6 cm)
1″(2.5 cm)

VIEW ON FRONT

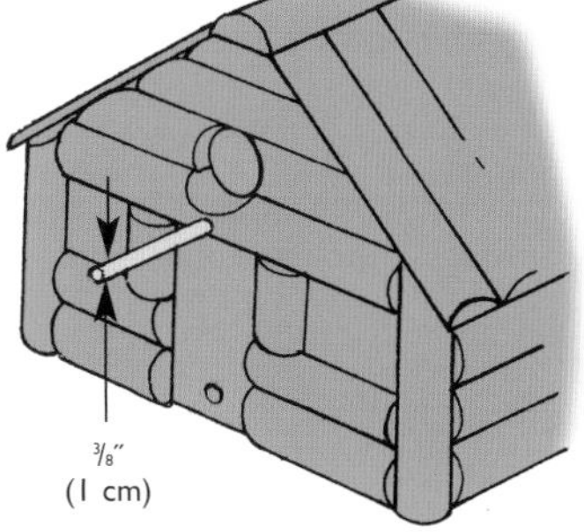
3/8″
(1 cm)

Prairie House (continued)

BASEBOARD

14. Cut the baseboard to size 14″ x 18″ (35.6 cm x 45.7 cm) from ½″ (1.3 cm) plywood and round the four corners. Mark out and cut the two support brackets from ¾″ (1.9 cm) wood. Screw the two pieces together and position them on the underside of the baseboard. Drill through the baseboard and glue and screw the battens to the underside.

15. Cut the ¾″ x ¾″ (1.9 cm x 1.9 cm) rear locating batten to fit the full internal width of the house. Screw this batten centrally, 1 ½″ (3.8 cm) from the rear edge. Cut the front-locating block and drive a 1 ½″ (3.8 cm) brass screw into the center of the front face, leaving ¾″ (1.9 cm) of the shank protruding. Cut the head off the screw with a junior hacksaw and file the edge smooth. To mark the hole position for the locating stud, rub a pencil point against the end of the screw to leave graphite deposits. Center the outside face of the door on the stud and push the house against the stud end. Use a drill of equal diameter to the stud to drill the locating hole, after transferring the mark to the outside face.

HITCHING RAIL PERCH

16. Cut the rail to length from ¼″ (0.6 cm) diameter dowel. Cut two short lengths of ½″ (1.3 cm) diameter dowel (or square bead) and file a recess in one end of each to take the rail. Drill a pilot hole in the end of each post and drill and screw through the baseboard to secure them. To prevent the pins splitting the posts, drill fine pilot holes in the tops of the posts before gluing and pinning the rail to them.

FINISHING TOUCHES

17. After filling any defects and recessed pin and screw heads with epoxy filler, sand all surfaces smooth. Paint the outer walls and roof with exterior masonry paint.

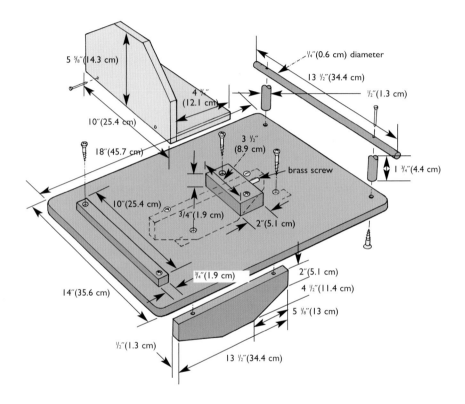

5 ⅝″ (14.3 cm)

¼″ (0.6 cm) diameter

13 ½″ (34.4 cm)

½″ (1.3 cm)

4 ¾″ (12.1 cm)

10″ (25.4 cm)

3 ½″ (8.9 cm)

brass screw

18″ (45.7 cm)

1 ¾″ (4.4 cm)

10″ (25.4 cm)

¾″ (1.9 cm)

2″ (5.1 cm)

¾″ (1.9 cm)

2″ (5.1 cm)

4 ½″ (11.4 cm)

5 ⅛″ (13 cm)

14″ (35.6 cm)

½″ (1.3 cm)

13 ½″ (34.4 cm)

Paddle House

MATERIALS

1 piece of 24″ x 12″ x ⅜″
(61 cm x 25.4 cm x 1 cm) plywood

1 piece of 18″ x 15″ x ½″ (45.7 cm x
38.1 cm x 1.3 cm) plywood

1 piece of 48″ x 3″ x ¾″
(121.9 cm x 7.6 cm x 1.9 cm) timber

Exterior wood glue

Stain and paint

¾″ (1.9 cm) molding pins

Screws

Terra-cotta dish

OTHER TOOLS

Router and ¼″ (0.6 cm) diameter
straight bit

Beam compass

MILL HOUSE

1. Draw the front entrance 3 ½″ x 2 ⅜″ (8.9 cm x 5.4 cm) on ⅜″ (1 cm) plywood, with a 45° roof pitch and 2 ⅜″ x 1 ½″ (5.9 cm x 3.8 cm) opening. Score across the grain and drill a ⅜″ (1 cm) diameter hole in the center waste. Use a jigsaw to cut the opening, inserting the blade through the hole. Finish the edges square with file or abrasive paper wrapped around a square batten. Cut around the outline and plane the edges square.

2. Draw the two pairs of side walls 2 ⅝″ x 1 ½″ (6.7 cm x 3.8 cm) and 5 ⅝″ x 3 ½″ (14.3 cm x 8.9 cm) on ⅜″ (1 cm) plywood. Score across the grain on each piece and cut each to size. Clamp each pair in the vise and plane the edges square.

3. Draw the front and rear walls 6 ½″ x 6″ (16.5 cm x 15.2 cm) on ⅜″ (1 cm) plywood, with a 45° roof pitch. Score across the grain on each piece and cut each to size. Clamp them together in the vise and plane to the same size, leaving the edges square. Cut out the opening in one piece to take the entrance. Do this with a jigsaw, finishing the internal edges square with a file or abrasive paper wrapped around a square batten.

4. Mark out the rebate on the edges of the front and back walls and the smaller side walls. The width of this rebate is equal to the thickness of the plywood (⅜″ (1 cm)) with a depth of two veneers or a third of the thickness of the edges.

5. Score across the grain on both pieces, before cutting on the inside of the line with a backsaw, to the rebate depth. Pare the plywood veneers away

with a chisel to form the rebates.

6. Glue and pin the sides together and check that the corners are square. When dry, plane or sand the edges flush and sink the pins with a punch.

7. Plane the top edges of the sides to follow the roof pitch. Cut two floors to size and angle the corners of the larger one. Glue and pin these into the mill.

ROOF

8. Mark out and cut the two L-shaped roof panels to size 6 ¾″ x 7″ (17.1 cm x 17.8 cm) from ⅜″ (1 cm) plywood. Clamp them in the vise together and plane them to the same size, leaving the edges square.

9. Draw a line across the inside face of the two pieces, ¼″ (0.6 cm) from the top edges and parallel. Plane to the line to leave a 45° miter. Glue these edges together to form the pitched roof. Cut a square batten to the internal length of the loft and position and glue it into the apex of the roof.

WHEEL

10. Using a pair of compasses, draw the two circular wheel rims 6 ¼″ (15.9 cm) diameter and backing plate 4 ¾″ (12.1 cm) diameter on ⅜″ (1 cm) plywood. Cut the wheel rims using the electric router fitted with a straight cutter and trammel point, or a jigsaw. The edges cut with the latter will need sanding.

11. To hold the plywood, fasten it to a waste board by pinning through the inner and outer waste and the rim itself. This will ensure that none of the pieces will move when cut free of each other. Check that none of the pins can be caught by the router cutter or saw blade, and, when using the router, cut in a series of shallow steps before cutting to the full depth. When cutting the spokes of the front rim, score along the lines before using the jigsaw, or clamp a straightedge across the wood to guide a router.

The New Birdhouse Book

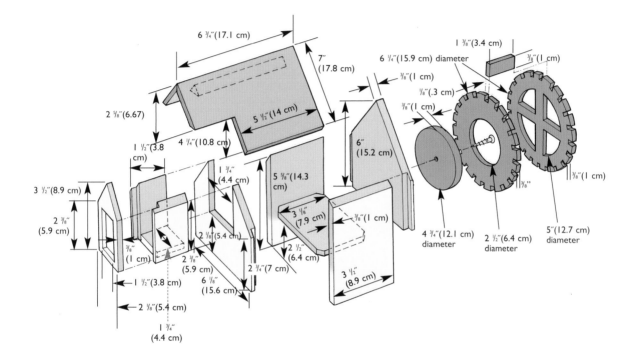

6 ¾"(17.1 cm)

7" (17.8 cm)

1 ⅜"(3.4 cm)

⅜"(1 cm)

6 ¼"(15.9 cm) diameter

⅛"(.3 cm)

⅜"(1 cm)

2 ⅝"(6.67)

5 ½"(14 cm)

⅜"(1 cm)

4 ¼"(10.8 cm)

1 ½"(3.8 cm)

6" (15.2 cm)

⅜"(1 cm)

3 ½"(8.9 cm)

1 ¾" (4.4 cm)

5 ⅝"(14.3 cm)

⅜"

2 ⅜" (5.9 cm)

2 ⅛"(5.4 cm)

3 ⅛" (7.9 cm)

⅜"(1 cm)

⅜"(1 cm)

2 ½" (6.4 cm)

5"(12.7 cm) diameter

4 ¾"(12.1 cm) diameter

2 ½"(6.4 cm) diameter

⅜" (1 cm)

2 ⅜" (5.9 cm)

2 ¾"(7 cm)

1 ½"(3.8 cm)

2 ⅜" (5.9 cm)

6 ⅛" (15.6 cm)

3 ½" (8.9 cm)

2 ⅛"(5.4 cm)

1 ¾" (4.4 cm)

Paddle House (continued)

12. Glue the backing plate to the rear rim. Mark out the spacing for 20 blades around the circumference of the front rim. Find the center of the rim with a pair of compasses and draw a circle on the face of the rim, 1/8″ (0.3 cm) from the edge, to mark the depth of the notches. Clamp both rims together in the vise, and use a try square to extend the center lines across the edge of both rims. From these lines, set out the width of each notch 3/32″ (0.2 cm).

13. Drill a 3/16″ (0.5 cm) hole at the center of the backing plate to take a round-headed brass mounting screw.

14. Use a fine backsaw to cut down either side of each notch. With a fret-saw or narrow chisel, cut out the waste from each notch.

15. Cut 20 1 1/4″ (3.2 cm) lengths of 1/4″ x 3/32″ (0.6 cm x 0.2 cm) strip (it may be necessary to plane thicker material to this size). Align the notices on both rims and clamp a 3/4″ (1.9 cm) batten between them. Glue as many of the blades to the rim before it is necessary to remove the batten. At this point allow the glue on the other slat to dry before releasing the clamps. Wipe any excess glue from both the inside and outside of the wheel.

BASEBOARD

16. Set out the size of the baseboard on 1/2″ (1.3 cm) plywood, using a 6″ (15.2 cm) diameter plate or paint can to draw the three large-radius corners. Use a large coin for the fourth quarter.

17. A shallow terra-cotta or plastic dish can be used for the birdbath, but do check that it has a ridged edge to allow it to sit level and securely in the circular cutout. Measure the diameter of the dish below the ridge level. Set out this diameter with a pair of compasses on the baseboard and check that there is room for the house and wheel.

18. Cut out the circle using either a jigsaw or a router fitted with a trammel bar. The latter will leave the best finish and save a lot cleaning up. Check that the dish fits before finally finishing the edge by sanding with abrasive paper over a curved backing block. Cut around the baseboard with a jigsaw, having first scored along the curved lines, and plane or sand the edge.

19. Mark out and cut the moat surround from 1/2″ (1.3 cm) plywood; sand all edges. Before painting the baseboard, temporarily screw the wheel to the mill and position the mill on the board. Position the moat under the wheel and glue it in the position.

20. After filling any defects and recessed pin and screw heads with epoxy filler, sand all surfaces smooth. Paint the roof and walls with exterior masonry paint. The water wheel and baseboard can be finished with a suitable nontoxic exterior-grade varnish or stain.

21. Cut the post brackets from a piece of 2 3/4″ x 3/4″ (7 cm x 1.9 cm) wood, cutting away the top edge to clear the dish. Screw the brackets and spacers together and screw the assembled bracket to the underside of the board.

22. Finally, screw the water wheel to the mill and screw the mill in place on the baseboard.

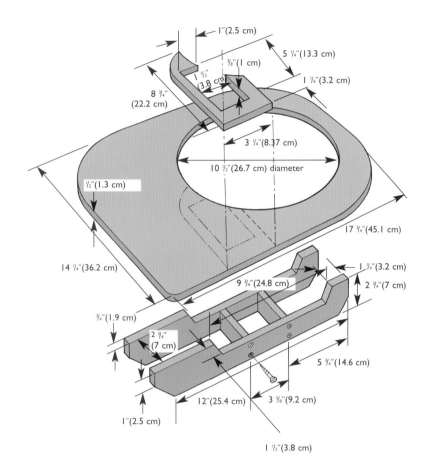

1"(2.5 cm)

³⁄₈"(1 cm)

5 ¹⁄₄"(13.3 cm)

1 ¹⁄₄"(3.2 cm)

1 ¹⁄₂"
(3.8 cm)

8 ³⁄₄"
(22.2 cm)

3 ¹⁄₄"(8.37 cm)

10 ¹⁄₂"(26.7 cm) diameter

¹⁄₂"(1.3 cm)

17 ³⁄₄"(45.1 cm)

14 ¹⁄₄"(36.2 cm)

9 ³⁄₄"(24.8 cm)

1 ¹⁄₄"(3.2 cm)

2 ³⁄₄"(7 cm)

³⁄₄"(1.9 cm)

2 ³⁄₄"
(7 cm)

5 ³⁄₄"(14.6 cm)

12"(25.4 cm)

3 ⁵⁄₈"(9.2 cm)

1"(2.5 cm)

1 ¹⁄₂"(3.8 cm)

Amish Nest Box

FRONT AND BACK

1. Draw the front and back panels onto ⅜″ (1 cm) plywood, setting out the curved top with a pair of compasses.

2. Score across the grain on both pieces and cut out with a jigsaw. Clamp the two pieces in the vise together. Finish the straight edges with a plane and the curved section with a rasp, or a sanding block and abrasive paper.

3. Cut the entrance hole with a hole-saw of 1″ to 1 ¼″ (2.5 cm to 3.2 cm) to suit the specific bird species. If required, cut a 2″ (5.1 cm) length of ¼″ (0.6 cm) diameter dowel and glue it into a hole drilled beneath the entrance hole. On the rear panel cut the V-shaped cutout.

4. Alternatively, a small platform can be screwed to the front of the box with a short bead fitted to its edge. To shelter the entrance hole, cut a small piece of plywood and bevel the rear edge. Fasten it above the entrance hole by screwing through from the back of the front panel.

5. Cut a piece of ⅛″ (0.3 cm) plywood with the face grain running across the narrow width.

6. Mark the very center of the top of the arch on the front and rear panels and draw a center line across the width of the roof panel.

7. Run a ribbon of glue around the edges of the rear panel. Drive a pin through the top panel on the center line (either on the edge or set 1″ (2.5 cm) back from the edge if an overhang is required). Align the center line on the roof panel with the center line on the rear panel and gently bend the plywood around the curved top edge. Use C-clamps, a webbing clamp, or cord tourniquet to gradually pull it down evenly, while securing it with pins.

8. Cut three blocks of wood equal in length to the final internal width of the box and stand them against the internal sides. Run a ribbon of glue around the edges of the front panel and rest it on top of the three blocks. Secure the front panel into the box as before.

9. When dry, plane the bottom edges flush and, if the front edge overhangs, round the bottom front corners of the curved panel.

10. The top of the box is designed to lift off its mounting bracket, leaving the nest base. Cut the mounting bracket from either a piece of 3″ × 1″ (7.6 cm × 2.5 cm) wood or as a ⅜″ (1 cm) plywood plate. Cut the plate to size and cut the ends or corners round.

11. Cut two triangular plates, one to fit into the V-shaped cutout in the back of the box, the other wider by ¼″ (0.6 cm) on each edge. Alternatively, battens can be screwed to the edges of the smaller plate. The base of the nesting box is cut to fit its internal dimensions from ⅜″ (1 cm) plywood. Cut out the base and round the corners. Glue and pin the base to the top triangular plate or to two short battens glued and pinned to the smaller one.

FINISHING TOUCHES

12. After filling any defects and recessed pin and screw heads with epoxy filler, sand all surfaces smooth. Paint the outer walls, roof, and base with a water-based stain, varnish, or masonry paint.

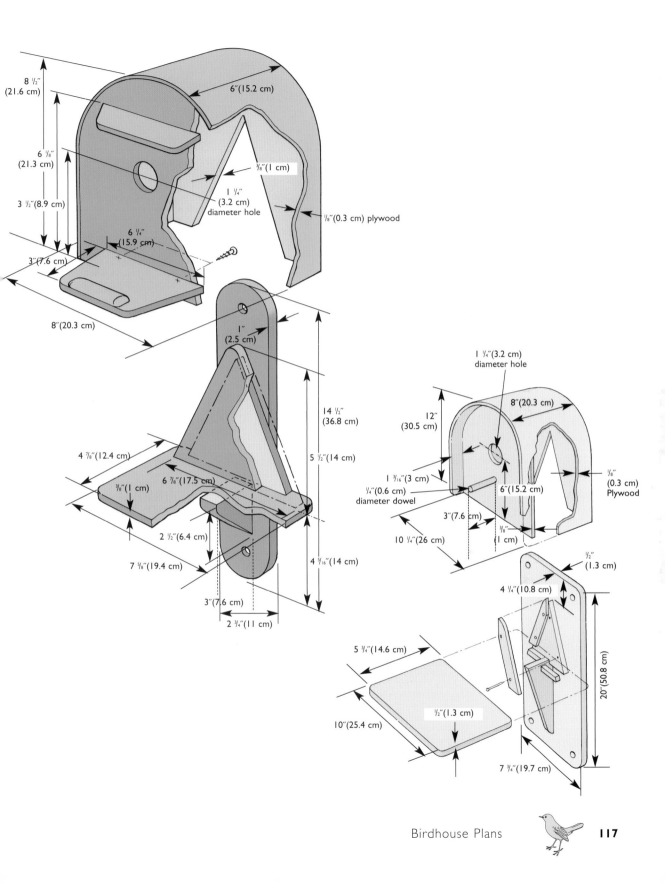

8 ½" (21.6 cm)

6" (15.2 cm)

6 ⅛" (21.3 cm)

⅜" (1 cm)

3 ½" (8.9 cm)

1 ¼" (3.2 cm) diameter hole

⅛" (0.3 cm) plywood

6 ¼" (15.9 cm)

3" (7.6 cm)

8" (20.3 cm)

1" (2.5 cm)

14 ½" (36.8 cm)

4 ⅞" (12.4 cm)

5 ½" (14 cm)

⅜" (1 cm)

6 ⅞" (17.5 cm)

2 ½" (6.4 cm)

7 ⅝" (19.4 cm)

4 ⁵⁄₁₆" (14 cm)

3" (7.6 cm)

2 ¾" (11 cm)

1 ¼" (3.2 cm) diameter hole

8" (20.3 cm)

12" (30.5 cm)

1 ³⁄₁₆" (3 cm)

¼" (0.6 cm) diameter dowel

6" (15.2 cm)

⅛" (0.3 cm) Plywood

3" (7.6 cm)

⅜" (1 cm)

10 ¼" (26 cm)

½" (1.3 cm)

4 ¼" (10.8 cm)

20" (50.8 cm)

5 ¾" (14.6 cm)

½" (1.3 cm)

10" (25.4 cm)

7 ¾" (19.7 cm)

Birdhouse Plans

117

Wild West House

MATERIALS

1 piece of 48″ × 24″ × ⅜″
(121.9 cm × 61 cm × 1 cm) plywood

1 piece of 21 ¾″ × 18″ × ⅛″ (55.2
cm × 45.7 cm × 0.3 cm) plywood

1 piece of 12″ × ⅜″ × ⅛″ (30.5 cm ×
1 cm × 0.3 cm) timber bead

1 piece of 18″ × 2 ¾″ × ¾″
(45.7 cm × 5.7 cm × 1.9 cm) timber

1 piece of 60″ × ¼″ × ¼″ (152.4 cm
× 0.6 cm × 0.6 cm) timber bead

1 piece of 60″ × ⅜″ × ⅜″ (152.4 cm
× 1 cm × 1 cm) timber bead

Exterior wood glue

Screws

Stain and paint

¾″ (1.9 cm) molding pins

OTHER TOOLS

Webbing clamps

Beam compass

Lathe

Router

1. From ¼″ (0.6 cm) plywood, cut two 8″ × 8 ½″ (20.3 cm × 21.6 cm) and one 8″ × 9 ⅛″ (20.3 cm × 23.2 cm) panels. On each panel, draw crossed center lines. On one panel only, use a pair of compasses to swing an 8″ (20.3 cm) diameter circle from the center point. Along one edge measure 3 ⅜″ (8.4 cm) on either side of the center line. Draw a line from the two points, meeting the circle at a tangent on either side.

2. Use a craft knife to score the full length of the line before cutting along the waste side with a jigsaw.

3. Lay the cut panel over the others in turn and draw around it. Cut the other panels to the same curve.

4. At the center of the two smaller panels cut a 1 ¼″ (3.2 cm) diameter entrance hole.

5. On the center panel cut a 1 ⅛″ × ¾″ (2.9 cm × 1.9 cm) notch at each corner.

6. From ⅛″ (0.3 cm) plywood cut a 21 ¾″ × 18″ (55.2 cm × 45.7 cm) rectangular panel with the grain running along the longer length. Draw a center line across the 18″ (45.7 cm) width and center lines for each of the three curved divisions, at rights angles to it.

7. Run a ribbon of glue along each center line. Align the top center of the middle curved division against the center line on the panel and pin the panel to it. Carefully wrap the plywood part way around the curve and secure with clamps or a cord tourniquet. Fit and pin the two end divisions in a similar manner. Working on one side at a time, tighten the plywood against the divisions, pinning it at 1″ (2.5 cm) intervals. Regularly tighten the clamps as you fasten further around the curve. Clean off any excess glue and leave the clamps in place until the glue has dried thoroughly.

8. To mark the splayed end of the canopy, wrap a strip of plastic or card around the curve at one end, positioning it against the edge at the top center. Pull the ends back to meet the bottom edge at a point ¼″ (0.6 cm) in front of the division. Draw a line along the edge of the strip and repeat the procedure at the other end. Score along the line and cut the splay with a fine-toothed backsaw.

9. After scoring with a craft knife, use a coping saw to trim the bottom edges of the two end divisions level, ⅜″ (1 cm) above the bottom edges of the curved top.

10. Cut two ⅜″ × ⅜″ (1 cm × 1 cm) strips and glue them along the bottom edge of the canopy.

11. On the inside ends of the canopy, glue two full-width battens ⅜″ × ⅛″ (1 cm × 0.3 cm), positioned to rest on the wagon ends when the canopy is fitted.

12. Cut two 7″ × 2 ⅛″ (17.8 cm × 5.4 cm) footboards from ⅜″ (1 cm) plywood and glue and pin them to the end panels of the canopy. Glue and pin a length of ¼″ (0.6 cm) diameter dowel to the front edge of each board.

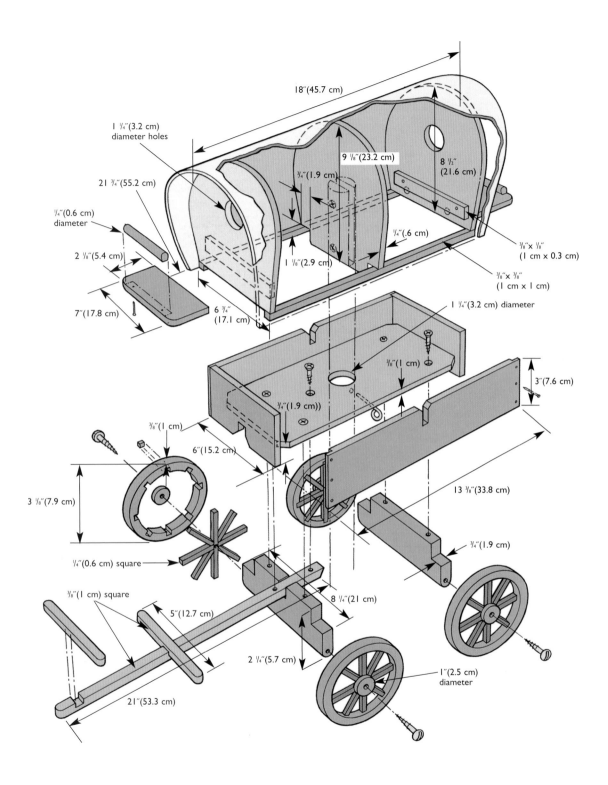

18"(45.7 cm)

1 1/4"(3.2 cm)
diameter holes

9 1/8"(23.2 cm)

8 1/2"
(21.6 cm)

21 3/4"(55.2 cm)

3/4"(1.9 cm)

1/4"(0.6 cm)
diameter

1/4"(.6 cm)

3/8"x 1/8"
(1 cm x 0.3 cm)

2 1/8"(5.4 cm)

1 1/8"(2.9 cm)

3/8"x 3/8"
(1 cm x 1 cm)

7"(17.8 cm)

6 3/4"
(17.1 cm)

1 1/4"(3.2 cm) diameter

3/8"(1 cm)

3"(7.6 cm)

3/4"(1.9 cm))

3/8"(1 cm)

6"(15.2 cm)

13 3/8"(33.8 cm)

3 1/8"(7.9 cm)

3/4"(1.9 cm)

1/4"(0.6 cm) square

3/8"(1 cm) square

5"(12.7 cm)

8 1/4"(21 cm)

2 1/4"(5.7 cm)

1"(2.5 cm)
diameter

21"(53.3 cm)

Wild West House (continued)

WAGON

13. Cut four strips of 3″ x ⅜″ (7.6 cm x 1 cm) plywood, two 13 ⅜″ (33.8 cm) long and two 6″ (15.2 cm) long. Mark out and cut ⅜″ x ³⁄₁₆″ (1 cm x 0.5 cm) rebates at the ends of the short lengths. Glue and pin the four pieces together, checking that the corners are square.

14. Cut the wagon floor from ⅜″ (1 cm) plywood and trim all four corners at 45° (for drainage). Glue the floor into the frame, raising it ¾″ (1.9 cm) up from the bottom edge.

15. Cut two 8 ¼″ x 2 ¼″ x ¾″ (21 cm x 5.7 cm x 1.9 cm) battens. Hold the battens in turn in a vise and round over one edge with a plane. Cut a notch at the end of each batten to allow them to be glued to the underside of the floor. On one batten, cut a notch, centered along the square edge, to allow the "trace" to pass through. Glue the battens in place.

16. Using the canopy as a guide, mark the position of the notches on both sides of the wagon to receive the center division when the canopy is fitted. Cut the notches and chamfer the top corners.

TRACES

17. Cut one 21″ x ⅜″ x ⅜″ (53.3 cm x 1 cm x 1 cm) and two 5″ x ⅜″ x ⅜″ (12.7 cm x 1 cm x 1 cm) battens. Along the longer piece, set out and cut two ⅜″ x ³⁄₁₆″ (1 cm x 0.5 cm) notches to take the short lengths, and glue and screw them in place. On the front of the wagon, cut a notch to allow the trace to be glued and screwed to the underside of the floor.

WHEELS

18. Mark out on ⅜″ (1 cm) plywood each of the four wheel rims and divide them into 12 equal segments. Mark out the width of each of the notches to take the spokes.

19. Cut out the wheel rims using the electric router fitted with a trammel point, set to a radius of 3 ⅛″ (7.9 cm). Reset the radius to leave a rim width of ⅝″ (1.6 cm) and cut the inner diameter. Remember to secure both the inner and outer waste as well as the rim before cutting.

20. With the rims clamped in the vise together, cut across the notches on all four at the same time, taking the waste out with a number of saw cuts. Square up the notches with a narrow file or chisel.

21. Cut the spoke to length from ¼″ (0.6 cm) square strip. The first spoke is glued into notches on opposite sides of the rim. The remaining spokes are cut and/or mitered to be glued at the center. The remaining part of the notch can be filled with epoxy filler and sanded. Turn four 1″ (2.5 cm) hob disks on a lathe or cut them from thin materials with a fretsaw. Glue each disk to the center of the spokes. Drill a hole through each hub to take a round-headed brass screw.

MOUNTING

22. Mount the wagon on a 3″ x 3″ (7.6 cm x 7.6 cm) post held by angle brackets or blocks screwed to the underside of the floor. Alternatively, drill a 1 ³⁄₁₆″ (3 cm) diameter hole through the underside of the wagon, to take an 18″ (45.7 cm) length of 1 ¼″ (2.9 cm) diameter dowel. Cut a 4″ x ⅜″ (10.2 cm x 1 cm) notch down the center of the dowel, and glue and screw it to the center division of the wagon. This allows the wagon to drop away from the canopy for cleaning out. Lift the wagon up tight beneath the canopy and mark the underside of the canopy. Remove the wagon and drill the dowel to take a ⅛″ (0.3 cm) diameter locking pin, made from bent brass rod or similar. Drill the top of the mounting post (3″ (7.6 cm) round or square) to allow the dowel to be inserted at least 5″ (12.7 cm). Secure the dowel in the post with a long wood screw.

FINISHING TOUCHES

23. After filling any defects and recessed pin and screw heads with epoxy filler, sand all surfaces smooth. Paint the canopy with exterior masonry paint and the wagon sides with a water-based stain or varnish.

**END AND CENTER
DIVISION DETAILS**

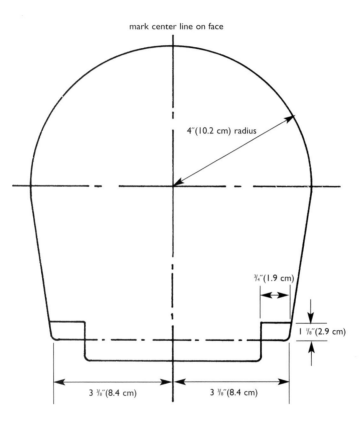

mark center line on face

4″(10.2 cm) radius

¾″(1.9 cm)

1 ⅛″(2.9 cm)

3 ⅜″(8.4 cm)

3 ⅜″(8.4 cm)

Little Boy Blue Nesting Box

MATERIALS

1 piece of 30″ x 24″ x ⅜″
(76.2 cm x 61 cm x 1 cm) plywood

1″ (2.5 cm) diameter wooden knob

1 piece of 80″ x ¼″ (203.2 cm x
0.6 cm) diameter dowel

Brass hooks and eyes

Exterior wood glue

Stain and paint

¾″ (1.9 cm) molding pins

TOP SECTION

1. Draw the four triangular segments of the top (base 11 ⅜″ x height 9 ⅝″ (28.8 cm x 24.4 cm)) on a piece of ⅜″ (1 cm) plywood with the grain running along their length and the wide and narrow ends alternated. Leave a gap of ⅛″ (0.3 cm) between each to allow for the width of the saw blade. Score across the grain along the angled edges before cutting.

2. Cut out each segment and mark one face of each. (This will be the inside face when the segments are glued together.) Stack all four together in a vise, and plane all to the same size with all the edges square.

3. Stand two of the sides together with their bases at 90° to each other. Measure the gap left between the two edges on the inside face. Draw a line parallel to the right-hand edge on each marked face, equal to this dimension. Plane a bevel down to this line on each of the four edges. Tape the pyramid together and check that each pair of edges mates along their full length. Glue and pin the joints together.

4. When dry, plane the joint edges flush and the bottom edge straight and level.

5. Cut the tip of the top pyramid to form a flat area and drill a ⅜″ (1 cm) hole. Glue a turned finial or knob into the hole.

BOTTOM SECTION

6. Draw the four triangular segments of the bottom base 9 ¼″ x height 8 ¼″ (24.8 cm x 21 cm) and repeat the procedure as for constructing the top.

7. Cut two squares of ⅜″ (1 cm) plywood 2 ¾″ x 2 ¼″ (7 cm x 7 cm) and 1 ½″ x 1 ½″ (3.8 cm x 3.8 cm). On one face of each, draw a line ¼″ (0.6 cm) from each edge. Plane a bevel along each edge finishing on the line.

8. Mark and drill a ½″ (1.3 cm) hole at the center of the smaller of the two squares, and glue the square into the pyramid. The second larger square is laid loose in the pyramid and forms the bottom of the box.

9. Cut a 1″ (2.5 cm) diameter entrance hole with a drill-mounted holesaw. Cut a 3″ (7.6 cm) length of ¼″ (0.6 cm) diameter dowel and glue it into a hole drilled beneath the entrance hole.

10. Screw two brass hooks on opposite sides of the bottom pyramid, to locate the screw eyes fitted to the underside of the top section.

MOUNTING

11. Cut the top of the bottom pyramid to form a flat area and drill a ½″ (1.3 cm) hole to take a ½″ (1.3 cm) diameter aluminum pole. Glue the pole into the base with an epoxy glue.

FINISHING TOUCHES

12. After filling any defects and recessed pin heads with epoxy filler, sand all surfaces smooth. Paint the outer walls, roof, and base with a water-based stain or nontoxic paint.

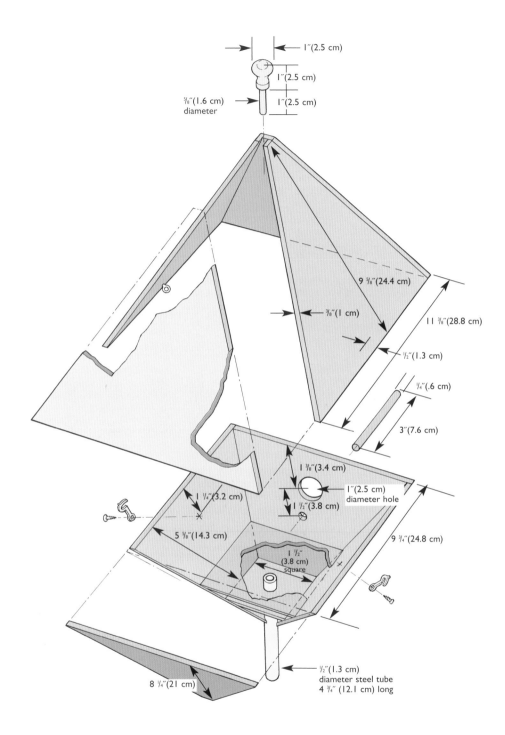

1"(2.5 cm)

1"(2.5 cm)

⅝"(1.6 cm)
diameter

1"(2.5 cm)

9 ⅝"(24.4 cm)

⅜"(1 cm)

11 ⅜"(28.8 cm)

½"(1.3 cm)

¼"(.6 cm)

3"(7.6 cm)

1 ⅜"(3.4 cm)

1"(2.5 cm)
diameter hole

1 ½"(3.8 cm)

5 ⅝"(14.3 cm)

1 ¼"(3.2 cm)

9 ¾"(24.8 cm)

1 ½"
(3.8 cm)
square

½"(1.3 cm)
diameter steel tube
4 ¾" (12.1 cm) long

8 ¼"(21 cm)

Birdhouse Plans

Seaside Cottage Box

WALLS

1. Cut two 5 ½″ x 7″ (14 cm x 17.8 cm) and two 9 ½″ x 6 ¼″ (24.1 cm x 15.9 cm) piece from ¼″ (0.6 cm) plywood.

2. Clamp the two smaller panels in the vise and plane to same size, leaving the edges square.

3. Draw on the larger two the 45° roof pitch. Score across the grain and cut to this angle. Clamp together in the vise and plane to the same size, leaving the edges square.

4. Mark out the rebate on the vertical inside face of the front and the back. These are equal to the thickness of the plywood ¼″ (0.6 cm) on the inside face of the each piece and depth of ⅛″ (0.3 cm).

5. Score across the grain on both pieces, before cutting to the depth on the inside of the line. Pare the plywood veneers away with a chisel to form the rebates.

6. Pin the four walls together, checking the bottom edges are flush and the corners are square.

7. When dry, plane the top edge of the side walls to follow the front- and rear-wall roof angle.

8. Cut the floor from ¼″ (0.6 cm) plywood, to a push fit inside the walls. Plane the edges square and trim the corners at 45° (for drainage). Drill the four walls and screw the floor in place.

9. Draw a center line down the front face. Drill the entrance hole with a 1″–1 ¼″ (2.5 cm–3.2 cm) holesaw to suit a specific species.

ROOF

10. Cut the two 6″ x 8″ (15.2 cm x 20.3 cm) roof panels from ¼″ (0.6 cm) plywood. Clamp both together in the vise and plane to the same size, leaving the edges square.

11. On one face of each panel draw a line ¼″ (0.6 cm) from one long edge. Plane down to the line to produce a 45° bevel along the line.

12. Cut a 4 ¾″ x ½″ x ½″ (12.1 cm x 1.3 cm x 1.3 cm) triangular bead and glue it against the beveled edge of the panel, centered across the width. Glue and pin the panels together to form the pitched roof.

BARGEBOARDS

13. Cut four lengths of ⅛″ x 1″ x 5″ (0.3 cm x 2.5 cm x 12.7 cm) plywood. Divide each length into nine equal divisions ½″ (1.3 cm) apart and mark these with a pencil. At alternative divisions, drill a ⅛″ (0.3 cm) diameter hole, and at the others cut a semicircular cutout using a fretsaw or router cutter.

14. Cut the miters on each end of the strips, and glue to the underside ⅛″ (0.3 cm) back and parallel to the pitched edges of the roof.

MOUNTING

15. Mount this birdhouse in among the stems of a mature wisteria or other similar wall-climbing plant. Alternatively, it can be wall-mounted in a niche or on a simple bracket.

FINISHING TOUCHES

16. After filling any defects and recessed pin and screw heads with epoxy filler, sand all surfaces smooth. Paint the outer walls, roof, and base with nontoxic stain or varnish and paint the bargeboards white.

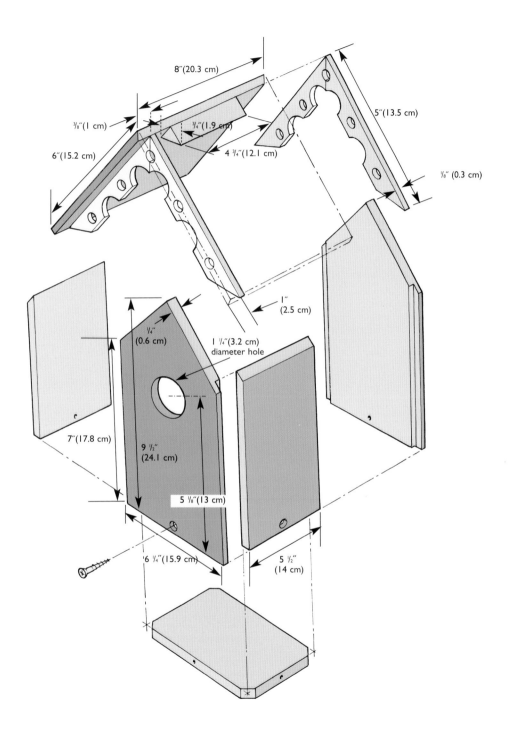

8″ (20.3 cm)

⅜″ (1 cm)

¾″ (1.9 cm)

5″ (13.5 cm)

6″ (15.2 cm)

4 ¾″ (12.1 cm)

⅛″ (0.3 cm)

1″ (2.5 cm)

¼″ (0.6 cm)

1 ¼″ (3.2 cm) diameter hole

7″ (17.8 cm)

9 ½″ (24.1 cm)

5 ⅛″ (13 cm)

6 ¼″ (15.9 cm)

5 ½″ (14 cm)

Birdhouse Plans **125**

Farmhouse Box

1. Draw out the two end walls, 5 ⅛″ (13 cm) wide by 6″ (15.2 cm) high, on ⅜″ (1 cm) plywood. Set out the 45° roof angle and score across the grain before cutting. Clamp both pieces together in the vise and plane to the same size, leaving all the edges square.

2. Draw out the front and rear walls, 10 ¼″ (26 cm) wide and 4″ (10.2 cm) high, on ⅜″ (1 cm) plywood. Set out the window and door positions and score across the grain before cutting. Clamp both together in the vise and plane to the same size, leaving the edges square. Plane the top edge at an angle of 45°.

3. Mark out the rebate on the vertical inside face of the front and back. These are equal to the thickness of the plywood (⅜″ (1 cm)) on the inside face of each piece, with a depth of ³⁄₁₆″ (0.5 cm).

4. Draw a center line down the front face and cut the entrance hole with a 1″–1 ¼″ (2.5 cm–3.2 cm) holesaw to suit the specific species.

5. Score across the grain on both pieces, before cutting with a backsaw to the full depth on the inside of the line. Pare the plywood veneers away with a chisel to form the rebates.

6. Glue and pin the four walls together, checking that the bottom edges are flush and that the corners are square.

ROOF

7. From ⅜″ (1 cm) plywood, cut two 11 ¼″ x 4 ⅝″ (28.6 cm x 11.7 cm) roof panels and score across the grain. Cut out both sections, clamp them together in the vise and plane to the same size, leaving the edges square. Cut two 90° triangular pieces of ¼″ (0.6 cm) plywood 3″ (7.6 cm) wide.

8. Along one edge on each end section, plane a 45° angle. Glue and pin the two sections together. When dry, position the roof on the walls and mark out the angled ends. Hold the work in a vise and score across the grain before cutting to the lines. Sand the cut edges flat and glue two triangular plates across the angles. When dry, sand or plane the edges flush with the roof surface.

9. Position the roof on the walls and mark the position and width of the windows along the front edge. Mark the line of the front wall on the underside of the roof. Use a try square to continue these positions up the underside of the roof slope beyond the eaves and thickness of the wall. Draw a line ¼″ (0.6 cm) back from the inside wall, score across the grain, and cut out the dormer window openings in the roof.

10. From ¼″ (0.6 cm) plywood, cut the two dormer window roof panels 2 ½″ long x 1 ½″ (6.4 cm x 3.8 cm) wide. Measure ⅝″ (1.6 cm) along from each end but on opposite edges, and draw a line across the faces. Score and cut along the line. Along the meeting edges of the roof panels, plane a 45° angle and glue them together. When dry, sand the rear edge of each roof until these sit flat against the face of the main roof.

WINDOWS AND DOOR

11. Cut two pieces of ¼″ (0.6 cm) plywood, 2″ (5.1 cm) wide and 7″ (17.8 cm) long. On one end of each mark the center and cut at 45° angle to either side. Cut the edges of the strip to allow it to slide up the dormer roof. Check that the angle fits to the underside of the dormer roof.

12. Repeat this on the other strip and, with the roof on the walls, glue both in position. Cut a blank piece of plywood larger than the door opening and glue it to the rear face of the wall over the door opening.

13. Cut the two ¾″ x 1 ¾″ (1.9 cm x 4.4 cm) sides of the porch roof, from ¼″ (0.6 cm) plywood, and plane one end of each to an angle of 45°. Glue these faces together and glue the porch to the wall face above the door.

BASEBOARD AND MOUNTING

14. Cut the 8″ x 12 ½″ (20.3 cm x 31.8 cm) baseboard from ⅜″ (1 cm) plywood and radius the corners. Position the walls on the board and mark the line of the inside face of the end walls. Screw two short battens against the lines. After painting, locate the cottage over the battens and screw through predrilled and countersunk holes in the end walls.

15. Cut out the two angle mounting plates from 5″ x 5″ x ⅜″ (12.7 cm x 12.7 cm x 1 cm) plywood. Cut a 5″ x 1 ½″ x 1 ½″ (12.7 cm x 3.8 cm x 3.8 cm) long block and glue and screw the two plates either side of it. Mount the cottage on a 1 ½″ (3.8 cm) square post, fitted between the plates and held by two screws from each face.

FINISHING TOUCHES

16. After filling any defects and recessed pin and screw heads with epoxy filler, sand all surfaces smooth. Paint the outer walls and roof with masonry paint and finish the baseboard with a water-based stain.

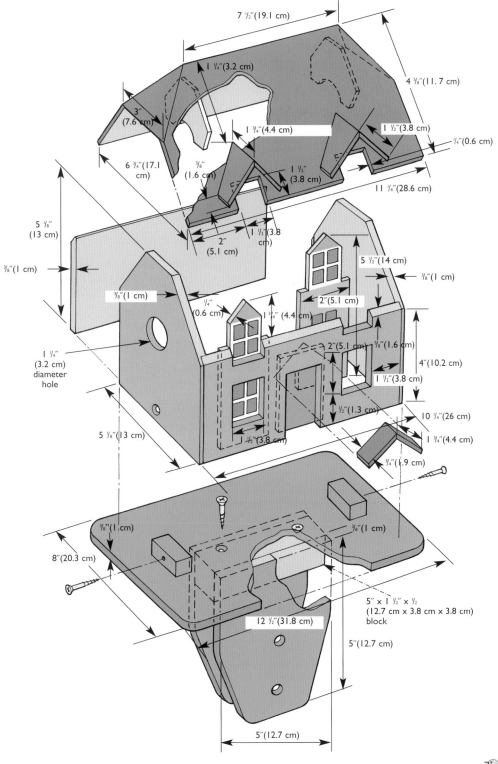

7 1/2"(19.1 cm)

1 1/4"(3.2 cm)

4 5/8"(11.7 cm)

3"
(7.6 cm)

1 3/4"(4.4 cm)

1 1/2"(3.8 cm)

1/4"(0.6 cm)

6 3/4"(17.1 cm)

5/8"
(1.6 cm)

1 1/2"
(3.8 cm)

11 1/4"(28.6 cm)

5 1/8"
(13 cm)

3/8"(1 cm)

3/8"(1 cm)

2"
(5.1 cm)

1 1/2"(3.8 cm)

5 1/2"(14 cm)

3/8"(1 cm)

1/4"
(0.6 cm)

2"(5.1 cm)

1 3/4" (4.4 cm)

1 1/4"
(3.2 cm)
diameter
hole

2"(5.1 cm)

5/8"(1.6 cm)

4"(10.2 cm)

1 1/2"(3.8 cm)

1/2"(1.3 cm)

10 1/4"(26 cm)

1 3/4"(4.4 cm)

5 1/8"(13 cm)

1 1/2"(3.8 cm)

3/4"(1.9 cm)

3/8"(1 cm)

3/8"(1 cm)

8"(20.3 cm)

5" x 1 1/2" x 1/2"
(12.7 cm x 3.8 cm x 3.8 cm)
block

12 1/2"(31.8 cm)

5"(12.7 cm)

5"(12.7 cm)

Circus Tent

MATERIALS

1 piece of 30″ x 20″ x ¼″
(76.2 cm x 50.8 cm x 0.6 cm) plywood

1 piece of 4″ x 4″ x 2″
(10.2 cm x 10.2 cm x 5.1 cm) timber

1 piece of 1 ½″ x ¼″
(3.8 cm x 0.6 cm) diameter dowel

Exterior wood glue

Stain/varnish

¾″ (1.9 cm) molding pins

1 wooden bead

SIDES

1. Cut the six 10 ½″ x 5 ½″ (26.7 cm x 14 cm) sides from ¼″ (0.6 cm) plywood and mark one face of each. (This will be the inside face when the sides are glued together.) Stack all six together in a vise, and plane all to the same size, leaving all the edges square.

2. Use a sliding bevel to accurately mark a 60° angle on one edge of two of the sides and draw a line between the points across the face. Bevel the edges of these two sides by planing down to the line, taking care not to decrease their width. Use this angle as a guide and adjust it by planing a fine shaving from the edge, until each pair of edges mate along the full length of the joint, with their bases set at an agle of 120°.

3. Measure the distance of the planed line from the edge and mark the other pieces in a similar fashion. Check that each joint mates along its full length.

4. Draw a center line down the front face of one side. Cut the entrance hole with a holesaw, depending on the size of the bird species you wish to attract.

5. Glue and tape the six sides together, checking that each opposite pair of sides is parallel and the diagonal dimensions are equal.

6. Draw a hexagon on a piece of ½″ (1.3 cm) plywood less than the internal hexagonal base of the tent. With a sliding bevel, measure the vertical angle of the tent sides and plane the edges of the base to this angle. Check that the base fits into the tent leaving a lip of around ½″ (1.3 cm). Glue the base into the tent.

7. When dry, stand the tent on a flat surface and draw a level line around the base. Hold the tent in a vise and plane down to the line, leaving a lip of about ³⁄₁₆″ (0.5 cm). Plane the top edge level in a similar way.

8. Cut six triangular sides from ⅛″ (0.3 cm) plywood and mark one face of each. (This will be the inside face when the

segments are glued together.) Stack all six together in a vise, and plane all to the same size leaving all the edges square.

9. Use a sliding bevel to accurately mark a 60° angle on one edge of two of the sides and draw a line between the points across the face. Bevel the edge of these two sides by planing down to the line, taking care not to decrease their width to any great extent. Use this angle as a guide and adjust it by planing a fine shaving from the edge, until each pair of edges mate along the full length of the joint, with their bases set at an angle of 120°. Glue and tape the pieces together, checking that they meet correctly at the top.

10. Measure the internal size of the hexagonal opening in the top of the tent. Draw out a hexagon to this size, on a piece of 2″ (5.1 cm) thick wood. Plane the edges around one face to the internal angle of the roof. Glue the hexagonal block into the roof.

11. Drill a ¼″ (0.6 cm) diameter hole through the apex of the roof into the block. Glue a 3″ x ¼″ (7.6 cm x 0.6 cm) length of dowel into the hole and glue a plastic or wooden bead to the top.

FINISHING TOUCHES

12. After filling any defects and recessed pin holes with epoxy filler, sand all surfaces smooth. Paint the outer walls with a differently colored water-based stain, masking the edges of each strip in turn with masking tape. Finally apply a coat of a clear, water-based, exterior-grade varnish over the external surfaces.

MOUNTING

13. Mount this birdhouse in among the stems of a mature wisteria or other similar wall-climbing plant. Alternatively, it can be wall-mounted in a niche or bracket, or on a post. To fix it securely, screw a small wooden block or metal (brass or aluminum) angle to the underside.

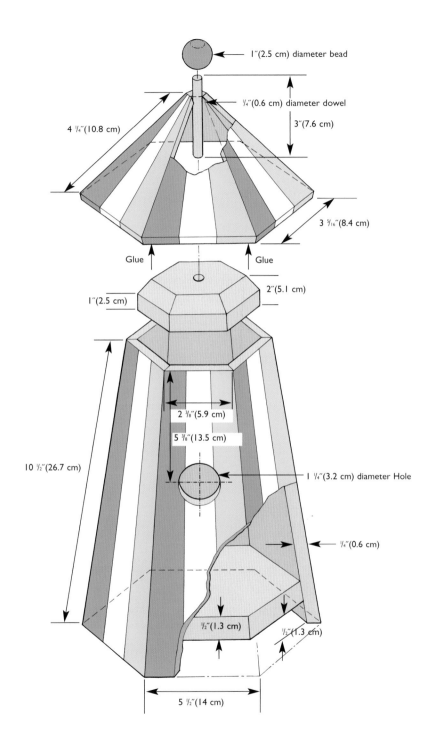

1"(2.5 cm) diameter bead

¼"(0.6 cm) diameter dowel

3"(7.6 cm)

4 ¼"(10.8 cm)

3 ⁵⁄₁₆"(8.4 cm)

Glue

Glue

2"(5.1 cm)

1"(2.5 cm)

2 ³⁄₈"(5.9 cm)

5 ³⁄₈"(13.5 cm)

1 ¼"(3.2 cm) diameter Hole

10 ½"(26.7 cm)

¼"(0.6 cm)

½"(1.3 cm)

½"(1.3 cm)

5 ½"(14 cm)

Secret Garden Nest Box

MATERIALS

1 piece of 52″ x 48″ x 3/8″ (132.1 cm x 121.9 cm x 1 cm) plywood

1 piece of 72″ x 1″ x 1/2″ (182.9 cm x 2.5 cm x 1.3 cm) plywood

1 length 12″ (30.5 cm) wide aluminum self-adhesive flashing material

Exterior wood glue

Stain and paint

3/4″ (0.6 cm) molding pins

Screws

WALLS

1. Cut six 7″ x 7″ (17.8 cm x 17.8 cm) wall segments to size from 3/8″ (1 cm) plywood and mark one face of each (the inside face when the segments are glued together). Stack all six together in a vise, and plane to the same size, leaving all the edges square.

2. Use a sliding bevel to accurately mark the 60° angle on the edges of the piece and draw lines across the marked face. Bevel the edge of each segment by planing down to the line, taking care not to decrease the width.

3. Tape the six segments together and stand them on a piece of 1/2″ (1.3 cm) plywood. Check that each pair of sides is equidistance and parallel. Draw along the inside edges to mark out the internal hexagonal shape on the plywood.

4. Score along any pencil lines that run across the grain, before cutting out the internal base. Make sure you cut along the outside of the lines. Otherwise, the base will be too small.

5. Mark out the center point of the entrance hole on one of the segments, and cut the hole using a holesaw held in a drill.The size of the hole should be chosen to suit the species that you are hoping to attract.

6. Draw a line 1/8″ (0.3 cm) up from the bottom edge of the inside face of each segment. Glue and pin each segment to the base, applying glue at each edge joint in turn. Align the bottom edges of the base with the line drawn on the segments, to leave a lip. Use a piece of string as a tourniquet, to pull the edge joints together and secure with tape until dry.

ROOF

7. Draw the six triangular roof segments (base 8″ x height 16″ (20.3 cm x 40.6 cm)) on a piece of plywood with the grain running along their length and the wide and narrow ends alternated. Leave a gap of 1/8″ (0.3 cm) between each to allow for the width of the saw blade. Score across the grain along the long edges before cutting out.

8. Cut out each segment and mark one face of each. (This will be the inside face when the segments are glued together.) Stack all six together in a vise, and plane all to the same size with all the edges square.

9. On the abutting edges of two of the segments, mark a 60° angle and join them with a line drawn across the inside face. The actual finished angle will be slightly more than 60°, but this will provide a good guide to work to.

10. Bevel the edges of the two segments by planing down to the line, taking care not to decrease the width of each piece. Check and adjust the angle by lightly planing until their faces mate along their full length when their bases are set at an angle of 120° (angle at which the walls meet). Set a bevel gauge to the finished edge angle and mark and plane the remaining segment edges to this angle. Mark this angle (x) on a piece of scrap wood for reference when cutting the edge bead (step 16).

11. Tape the roof segments together and set the sliding bevel to the roof pitch angle. Mark this angle (y) on a piece of scrap wood for reference when cutting edge bead (step 14).

12. Glue and pin the segments together, applying glue to each edge joint in turn and taping them until the glue has dried.

13. Mark out and cut a hexagon from a piece of 3/8″ (1 cm) plywood, 3/4″ (1.9 cm) smaller than the base of the roof. Mark out and plane the edges of the hexagonal piece to the roof angle.When the roof is dry, check that the hexagon fits into it, leaving at least a 1″ (2.5 cm) lip from the bottom edge, before gluing it in place. Check that it lies parallel to the bottom edge on all sides. When dry, plane the edge joints flush with the face of each roof segment.

14. Plane one edge of a length of 1″ x 1/2″ (2.5 cm x 1.3 cm) batten to match the roof pitch angle (y) (see step 11). Mark out the length of the bottom edge of one roof segment along the angled edge of the batten. Set the sliding bevel to the roof segment edge angle (x) and mark the angle at each end of the length. Mark out six pieces in this way, but cut them all slightly over length. Use a sharp chisel or sanding disk to trim end angle to allow the end of each bead to mate when fitted around the bottom edge of the roof. Glue and clamp each piece in place until dry.

15. Trim the beads to meet equally around the roof and trim and round over the point at the top.

16. Hold the completed wall section firmly in a vise or clamped to a bench. Plane the top edge of each wall segment to match the roof pitch angle (x) (see step 11).

WINDOWS AND DOOR FRAMES

17. On thin plywood, mark out the arched door and window frames, and score the curved edges. Mark out the position of each on the walls.

18. Cut out each piece and glue in position on the walls. Cut two lengths of bead to form the windowsills. Round over each end and glue each in place.

BASEBOARD

19. Mark out and cut the hexagonal baseboard (17″ (43.2 cm) measured across the flats) from 1/2″ (1.3 cm) plywood and plane each edge straight and square.

20. Position the wall section on the base, and draw round it. Cut two 4″ x 1″ x 3/8″ (10.2 cm x 2.5 cm x 1 cm) spacers and glue and screw them to the baseboard within the wall area. (The spacers lift the house to prevent rainwater from being trapped underneath.)

21. Mark out and cut the floor support brackets from a piece of 3/4″ (1.9 cm) wood. Screw the four pieces together and position them on the underside of the baseboard. Drill through the baseboard and glue and screw the battens to the underside.

ROOF COVERING

22. For the roof covering we have used bitumen-backed simulated-lead-finish aluminum foil. This is a self-adhesive material available from builders' merchants and similar stores. Take care when rolling out the foil to avoid creasing it too much.

23. Draw out and cut paper patterns for the top and bottom pieces of foil, leaving adequate margins for trimming. Using a craft knife and steel straightedge, cut out the six lower pieces. Warm the bitumen gently with a hot-air gun, before applying the foil to the roof. Position the piece carefully and trim off the edges along the joint lines. Press the bottom edges to the back of the beads and wrap it over and under them. Trim it to the inside edge of the roof. Repeat this with each lower piece, before cutting and repeating the procedure for the top pieces. Leave an overlap of ³/₁₆″ (0.5 cm) between the top and lower pieces. Cut six ¼″ (0.6 cm) strips and fold and stick them over the edge joints. Cut a small hexagonal patch and lay this over the top and fold it down over the rounded point.

FINISHING TOUCHES

23. After filling any defects and recessed pin and screw heads with epoxy filler, sand all surfaces smooth. Paint the outer walls with exterior paint. Paint both the baseboard and support battens with a suitable nontoxic exterior-grade varnish or stain. Screw the house in place over the spacers ready for mounting on a square or round section post.

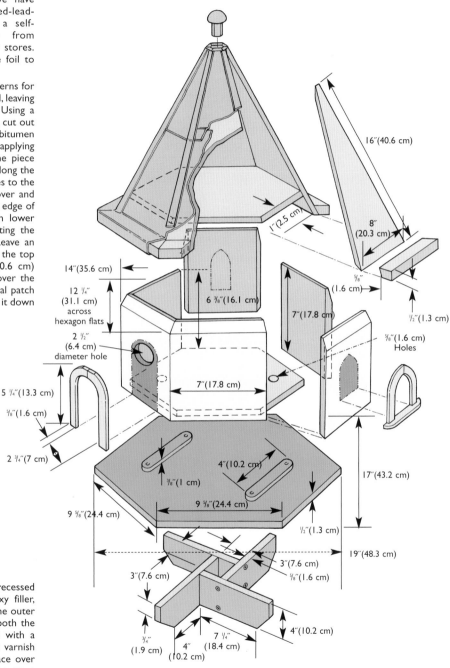

Pond House

MATERIALS

1 piece of 48″ x 36″ x ¾″ (121.9 cm x 91.4 cm x 1.9 cm) plywood

1 piece of 96″ x 6″ x ¾″ (243.8 cm x 15.2 cm x 1.9 cm) timber

1 piece of 72″ x 6″ x ¾″ (182.9 cm x 15.2 cm x 1.9 cm) timber

1 piece of 30″ x 4″ x ¾″ (76.2 cm x 10.2 cm x 1.9 cm) timber

1 piece of 24″ x ½″ x ¾″ (61 cm x 1.3 cm x 1.9 cm) timber

1 piece of 84″ x 1 ¾″ x 1 ¾″ (213.4 cm x 4.4 cm x 4.4 cm) timber

1 piece of 72″ x 2 ½″ x ¾″ (182.9 cm x 6.4 cm x 1.9 cm) timber

1 piece of 120″ x ½″ (304.8 cm x 1.3 cm) half-round bead

Exterior glue

Screws

¾″ (1.9 cm) molding pins

Paint

WALLS AND FRONT

1. Draw out the front and rear walls on ¾″ (1.9 cm) plywood. Score across the grain and use a jigsaw to cut around the undercuts. In case there is any variation in lumber sizes between suppliers, check that the board to be used will be a snug fit in the undercut and adjust accordingly. Take care to cut the edges straight, and square the edges with a plane or rasp. Paint the edges of plywood thoroughly to seal them.

2. Draw out the shape of the entrance hole on one panel. Score around the arch and drill a ⅜″ (1 cm) hole through the waste. Insert the jigsaw through the hole and cut on the waste side of the score line. Cut a 1 ½″ (3.8 cm) hole at the top of each panel.

3. Cut the two end boards from 4″ x ¾″ (10.2 cm x 1.9 cm) material to a length of 13 ½″ (34.3 cm) and mark out a ¾″ x ⅜″ (1.9 x 1 cm) rebate on each end.

4. Score across the rebate line on the face of the boards, and cut in both directions with a hacksaw.

5. Counterbore the screw holes to sink the screw heads and screw the end boards to the front and rear panels, aligning the bottom with the bottom edges of the panels.

6. Plane the excess wood away from the top of the board, leaving a beveled edge following the angle of the roof slate.

SLATTED ROOF

7. Cut four 6″ x ¾″ (15.2 cm x 1.9 cm) roof slats to a length of 22 ¾″ (57.8 cm) and set out the screw positions and counterbore the holes. Screw and glue the top two slats to the end panels, leaving a ¾″ (1.9 cm) overhang at the rear.

8. Cut a further four slats to a length of 15 ¼″ (38.7 cm) and set out the screw positions and counterbore the holes. Screw these boards to the end panels, leaving the same overhang at the back.

9. Cut a third panel from ¾″ (1.9 cm) plywood, similar to the other two but only 13″ (33 cm) wide. Drill the 1 ½″ (3.8 cm) hole as for previously cut panels.

10. Cut three 7″ (17.8 cm) wide pieces from ¾″ (1.9 cm) plywood, one 9 ½″ (24.1 cm) and two 22″ (55.9 cm) long. Cut two 9 ½″ (24.1 cm) lengths of 1″ x 1″ (2.5 cm x 2.5 cm) batten, and screw one to the face of the panel, 1″ (2.5 cm) below the entrance hole, and the other at a matching height on the rear face of the narrow panel. Screw the shorter of the 7″ (17.8 cm) panels between the two battens. Screw the top slats onto the angled shoulders of the narrower panel.

11. Plane one edge of the remaining slats to an angle of 45°. Screw these together along the beveled edges. Cut a 1 ½″ x 1 ½″ (3.8 cm x 3.8 cm) square batten to

fit between the two main end panels. Screw and glue the batten into the roof angle to position the ends of the lift-off section in line with the lower slats.

RAISED FLOOR

12. Cut four lengths of 1 ¾″ x 1 ¾″ (4.4 cm x 4.4 cm) lumber 12″ (30.5 cm) long. Set a sliding bevel to the internal angle between the end board and the lower slat, and cut one end of each leg to this angle. When assembled, the legs support the duck house with the underside of the lower slats resting on the beveled end. From the highest edge of the leg, measure down 3 ¾″ (9.5 cm) and draw a line across that face. Measure down a further 1 ¾″ (4.4 cm) for the halving joint, and set out its depth of ⅝″ (1.6 cm) on either side. Cut the halvings by making a series of cuts through the wood and chisel out the waste.

13. Cut the two cross rails to length to fit across the inside width of the house. Screw and glue and the rails into the halvings. Cut four 2 ½″ x ¾″ (6.4 cm) slats 22″ (55.9 cm) long. (Check that they are a clearance fit inside the house.) Screw and glue these to the cross rails leaving equal gaps between them.

14. The two entrance ramps are fitted by hinging them with a pair of back flap hinges (ideally brass), screwed to the underside of the ramp and the entrance step. Pin five equally spaced lengths of half-round bead across the ramp, sinking the pin heads so that they cannot work up above the surface and cause injury to the ducks.

FINISHING TOUCHES

15. After filling any defects and recessed pin and screw heads with epoxy filler, sand all surfaces smooth. Finish the outer walls and roof with nontoxic stain, varnish, or paint, and protect the inner parts of the legs with a water-based preservative.

The New Birdhouse Book

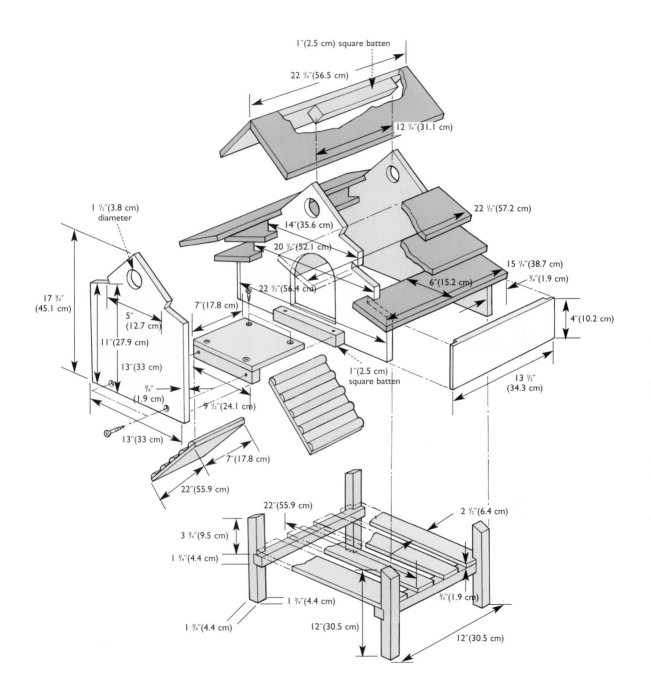

1″(2.5 cm) square batten

22 ¼″(56.5 cm)

12 ¼″(31.1 cm)

1 ½″(3.8 cm) diameter

22 ½″(57.2 cm)

14″(35.6 cm)

20 ½″(52.1 cm)

15 ¼″(38.7 cm)

6″(15.2 cm)

¾″(1.9 cm)

17 ¾″ (45.1 cm)

5″ (12.7 cm)

11″(27.9 cm)

13″(33 cm)

7″(17.8 cm)

22 ½″(56.4 cm)

4″(10.2 cm)

¾″ (1.9 cm)

13 ½″ (34.3 cm)

9 ½″(24.1 cm)

1″(2.5 cm) square batten

13″(33 cm)

7″(17.8 cm)

22″(55.9 cm)

22″(55.9 cm)

2 ½″(6.4 cm)

3 ¾″(9.5 cm)

1 ¾″(4.4 cm)

1 ¾″(4.4 cm)

¾″(1.9 cm)

1 ¾″(4.4 cm)

12″(30.5 cm)

12″(30.5 cm)

Purple Martin Apartment

MATERIALS

2 pieces of 132″ x 6″ x ¾″ (335.3 cm x 15.2 cm x 1.9 cm) timber

1 piece of 48″ x 3″ x ¾″ (121.9 cm x 7.6 cm x 1.9 cm) timber

1 piece of 36″ x 2″ x ¾″ (91.4 cm x 5.1 cm x 1.9 cm) timber

1 piece of 60″ x 36″ x ½″ (152.4 cm x 91.4 cm x 1.3 cm) plywood

1 piece of 4″ x 2″ (10.2 cm x 5.1 cm) sawn timber (x height of post required)

1 piece of 60″ x 1 ½″x 1 ½″ (152.4 cm x 3.8 cm 3.8 cm) timber

Exterior wood glue

Paint

Screws

(Pulley, rope, and cleat if hoist required)

1. Cut two 19″ (48.3 cm) lengths of 6″ x ¾″ (15.2 cm x 1.9 cm) wood and mark the inside face. Divide the inside faces into two and mark out a ¾″ x ⅜″ (1.9 cm x 1 cm) housing on each. On each end mark out a ¾″ x ⅜″ (1.9 cm x 1 cm) rebate.

2. Cut two 20 ¼″ (51.4 cm) lengths of 6″ x ¾″ (15.2 cm x 1.9 cm) wood and mark the inside face. Divide the inside face in three and mark out two ¾″ x ⅜″ (1.9 cm x 1 cm) housings on each. Equidistant between each halving, mark the center of the entrance holes.

3. Score the rebate lines and cut in both directions with a backsaw. Score and cut across the halving lines. Remove waste with a chisel.

4. Using a 2″ (5.1 cm) diameter holesaw, drill the entrance holes from both sides.

5. Along the bottom edge on the inside face of each piece cut a ⅝″ x ⅜″ (1.6 cm x 1 cm) rebate.

6. Cut two 18 ¼″ (46.4 cm) lengths of 5 ⅜″ x ¾″ (13.5 cm x 1.9 cm) wood. Divide one face on each into two and mark out a ¾″ x ⅜″ (1.9 cm x 1 cm) housing on each. Divide the other face into three and mark out two ¾″ x ⅜″ (1.9 cm x 1 cm) housings on each.

7. Temporarily clamp the six pieces together to form a square with the divisions in place.

8. Cut four 6 ¾″ (17.1 cm) lengths of 5 ⅜″ x ¾″ (13.5 cm x 1.9 cm) wood. On two of them, mark out two housing ½″ x ⅜″ (1.3 cm x 1 cm) on one face, 1″ (2.5 cm) either side of the center line.

9. Reassembly the compartments, gluing the division joints and gluing and screwing the rebated corner joints.

10. Cut two 19 ½″ (49.5 cm) lengths of 3″ x ¾″ (7.6 cm x 1.9 cm) wood. Round two corners on one edge to a radius of ¾″ (1.9 cm), and drill two ¾″ (0.6 cm) diameter holes through the full width, 3″ (7.6 cm) inward from each end.

11. Cut two 9 ¼″ x 20 ¼″ x ½″ (23.5 cm x 51.4 cm x 1.3 cm) plywood floor panels, place the edges square, and check that they fit into the bottom rebate. Along the meeting edge form a cutout around the center vent and post hole and the two mounting plate housings. Glue and screw the panels into the rebates and to the bottom edges of the compartment divisions.

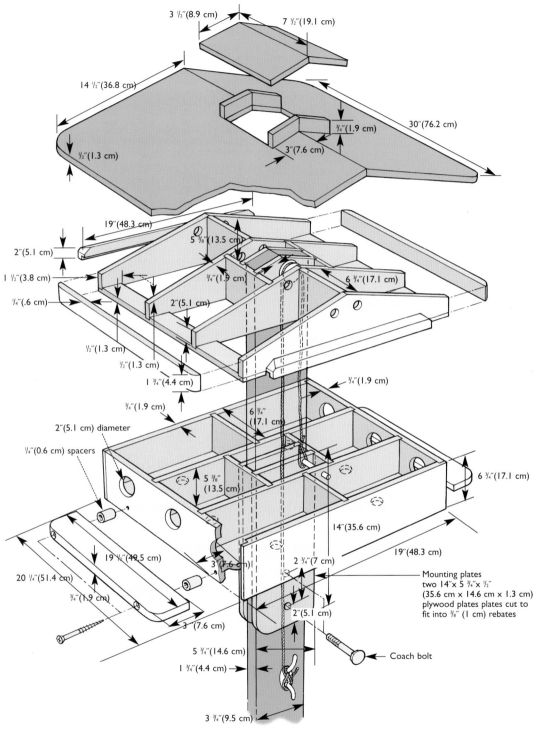

3 ½"(8.9 cm)

7 ½"(19.1 cm)

14 ½"(36.8 cm)

30"(76.2 cm)

¾"(1.9 cm)

½"(1.3 cm)

3"(7.6 cm)

19"(48.3 cm)

5 ⅜"(13.5 cm)

2"(5.1 cm)

6 ¾"(17.1 cm)

1 ½"(3.8 cm)

¾"(1.9 cm)

¼"(.6 cm)

2"(5.1 cm)

½"(1.3 cm)

½"(1.3 cm)

1 ¾"(4.4 cm)

¾"(1.9 cm)

¾"(1.9 cm)

2"(5.1 cm) diameter

6 ¾"
(17.1 cm)

¼"(0.6 cm) spacers

5 ⅜"
(13.5 cm)

6 ¾"(17.1 cm)

14"(35.6 cm)

19 ½"(49.5 cm)

19"(48.3 cm)

20 ¼"(51.4 cm)

3"(7.6 cm)

2 ¾"(7 cm)

¾"(1.9 cm)

Mounting plates
two 14"x 5 ¾"x ½"
(35.6 cm x 14.6 cm x 1.3 cm)
plywood plates plates cut to
fit into ⅜" (1 cm) rebates

2"(5.1 cm)

3" (7.6 cm)

5 ¾"(14.6 cm)

1 ¾"(4.4 cm)

Coach bolt

3 ¾"(9.5 cm)

Birdhouse Plans

135

Purple Martin Apartment (continued)

12. Cut two 5 ¾" x 14" x ½" (14.6 cm x 35.6 cm x 1.3 cm) plywood plates and form the stepped side edges to allow the plate to fit up into the housings. Glue the two plates into position.

ROOF

13. Cut four 22" (55.9 cm) lengths of 6" x ¾" (15.2 cm x 1.9 cm) wood. Mark out the roof angle on each, taking it from the center of the top edge to a point 43" (10.2 cm) down the end and cut along each piece. Clamp them together in vise, and plane them all to the same size, leaving the edges square. Either side of the center housing on each rafter, drill a ½" (1.3 cm) diameter ventilation hole.

14. Divide one face on each into two and mark out a ¾" x ⅜" (1.9 cm x 1 cm) housing on each. Divide the other face on two pieces into three and mark out two ¾"x ⅜" (1.9 cm x 1 cm) housings on each. Cut the housings as before.

15. Cut four 6 ¾" (17.1 cm) lengths of 5 ⅜" x ¾" (13.5 cm x 1.9 cm) wood. Clamp the frame together, and mark the beveled top edges of the short divisions. Cut and plane these to the correct height and angle. Glue and clamp the frame together, checking that the rafters are parallel. Between each housing drill a ½" (1.3 cm) hole.

16. Cut 1 ½" x ¼" (3.8 cm x .6 cm) rebates on the underside of each end of each rafter. Join the ends by gluing and screwing a 1 ½" x ½" (3.8 cm x 1.3 cm) batten into the rebates, checking that the rafters remain parallel to each other. Glue and pin a 1 ¾" x ¼" (4.4 cm x .6 cm) batten across the ends of the rafters and the edge of the bottom batten. (This will leave a narrow ventilation gap between the top edge of the batten and the underside of the roof.)

17. Cut the roof from two pieces of ½″ (1.3 cm) plywood, leaving an overhand of ½″ (1.3 cm) at the front and 2″ (5.1 cm) at either end. Use a sliding bevel to mark out the miter angle on both ends of each piece, and draw a line between the points. Plane a bevel along the edges, down to the line. Cut out the center section along the meeting edges for the raised vent and round the bottom corners of each piece. Glue and screw the roof onto the rafters.

18. Cut four 3″ x ½″ x ¾″ (7.6 cm x 1.3 cm x 1.9 cm) blocks and miter one end of each. Glue and pin the blocks to the roof at either end of the vent opening. Cut the two 7 ½″ x 3 ½″ x ½″ (19.1 cm x 1.3 cm x 1.3 cm) plywood vent panels and plane a miter along the one edge of each. Glue and pin the panels to the spacer blocks.

19. Cut two 19″ x 2″ x ¾″ (48.3 cm x 5.1 cm x 1.9 cm) battens and plane a bevel along one edge on each. Glue and pin these to the end of roof ends, to overlap the edge of ⅝″ (1.6 cm).

20. After filling any defects and recessed pin and screw heads with epoxy filler, sand all surfaces. Paint the roof with masonry paint.

21. Sand the two side perches, and prime and paint. Insert two 4 ¼″ (10.8 cm) coach screws through the holes and fit ¼″ (0.6 cm) spacers over the threads. Drill fine pilot holes in the sides of the house and screw the perches to it.

FINISHING TOUCHES

22. The mounting post or top section of the mounting post should be a snug fit into the post hole. Miter the top of the post to fit into the ventilation cap. When erected, the roof section can be screwed to the top, allowing the bottom section of the birdhouse to slide down the post of cleaning. The two plates are drilled to take a pair of coach bolts for locking the bottom section against the roof. For ease of use, a simply pulley system can be fitted to allow the bottom section to be lowered safely.

Birdhouse Plans **137**

Dovecote

MATERIALS

1 piece of 96″ × 48″ × ⅜″
(243.8 cm × 121.9 cm × 1 cm) plywood

1 piece of 48″ × 48″ × ½″
(121.9 cm × 121.9 cm × 1.3 cm)
plywood

1 piece of 144″ × 3″ × ¾″
(365.8 cm × 7.6 cm × 1.9 cm) timber

1 piece of 108″ × 3″ × ¾″
(274.3 cm × 7.6 cm × 1.9 cm) timber

1 piece of 72″ × 3″ × ¾″
(182.9 cm × 7.6 cm × 1.9 cm) timber

1 piece of 72″ × 2″ × ¾″
(182.9 cm × 5.1 cm × 1.9 cm) timber

1 piece of 18″ × 1″ × 1″
(45.7 cm × 2.5 cm × 2.5 cm) timber

Exterior wood glue

Screws

Stain and paint

¾″ (1.9 cm) molding pins

Finial

Post mounting bracket

COTE SIDES

1. Draw out a template of one of the side segments full size on a sheet of paper, taking the dimensions from our drawing. Start by drawing a center line on the sheet and measure half the width of the segment on either side of the line. The side angle will then be equal on either edge.

2. Cut out the template carefully. Set the template against the straight edges of a sheet of ⅜″ (1 cm) plywood and mark out the six segments from it.

3. After scoring across the grain, cut out each segment and mark one face of each. (This will be the inside face when the segments are glued together.) Stack all six together with one end held in a vise and the other clamped together and supported from underneath. (This is to prevent the sheets from dropping as they are being planed.) Plane all the same size, leaving the edges square.

4. To find the angle of the side panel edge joints, take two segments and mark the abutting vertical edges. On both edges of the piece, draw an angle of 60° toward the marked face. Join the lower points with a line drawn parallel to the edge.

5. Bevel the edges of the segment by planing down to the line, taking care not to decrease the width of the side. Check and adjust the angle by lightly planing until their faces mate along their full length when their bases are set at an angle of 120°. Set a bevel gauge to the finished edge angle and mark and plane the remaining segment edges to this angle.

6. Glue and pin each segment together, applying glue to each edge joint in turn and taping them until the glue dries. Check that each facing pair of segments is parallel and that the diagonal dimensions across the corners of the hexagon are equal.

7. On the face of each segment, draw a center line from top to bottom. Mark out the position and shape of the entrance holes, centering them on this line. Score across the grain, before cutting the holes

out with a jigsaw. Finish the edges of the entrance holes with a rasp and sanding with abrasive paper wrapped over a square block for the straight edges and a curved block for the arched tops.

8. Glue and pin the segments together in pairs, checking before joining the three pairs together, to complete the hexagon. Use strap clamps to hold the completed cote while the glue dries.

9. Cut three lengths of ¾″ × 2″ × 24″ (1.9 cm × 5.1 cm × 61 cm) batten. The narrow edges of these are to be planed to an angle of 60°. Mark the angle on both ends of the batten, on opposite faces (to form a rhombus). Draw, or scribe with a marking gauge, a line along the batten faces, parallel to the edges. Hold the batten in the vise and plane down to the line. Cut a 2″ × 1 ½″ (5.1 cm × 3.8 cm) length from the top of each and glue and clamp these blocks into the angle at the top of the vertical joints. When dry, plane the vertical joints flush.

PERCHES

10. With the cote standing on a flat surface, use a sliding bevel to take the vertical angle (x) of the sides.

11. Cut twelve 17″ (43.2 cm) lengths of 3″ × ¾″ (7.6 cm × 1.9 cm) wood. Transfer the vertical side angle to both ends of each piece and connect the lower points with a pencil or scribed line.

12. Hold the wood securely in a vise and plane a bevel down to the line.

13. Set the sliding bevel to an angle of 60° and transfer it to one end of each length of wood, splaying out from the bevel edge.

14. Cut the angle on one end of two of the lengths and check the miter against the base of the tapered sides. Lightly plane the miter faces to close any gaps. Hold the piece of wood, with the bevel edge against the base of the side, and mark the length. Set the sliding bevel to the adjusted angle (if necessary), and mark out and cut the angle. Glue and screw the lengths around the base of the dovecot and rill and screw through the side of the wood into the end of the mating board. This is to pull the joints tight. If any are cut too short, lightly plane the beveled edge.

15. Draw a line around the dovecote, 1″ (2.5 cm) below the upper entrance holes. To fit the high perch, position the top edge of the wood against the line as before.

16. As the perch widths may vary, choose the narrowest width, and draw a line equidistant from the side of the cote along the top face of each section. (These lines should all meet up at each end.) Plane the front edges of the perches to the line.

NESTING COMPARTMENTS

17. On the inside of the dovecote, measure the width of the sides at a point ½″ (1.3 cm) below the upper entrance holes. Use this dimension to set out the hexagonal floor of the upper compartment on a piece of ½″ (1.3 cm) plywood. In a similar manner, measure around the base at a point 1 ¼″ (3.2 cm) above the bottom edge and set out the lower hexagonal floor. Score across the grain and cut out both floors. Check that both floors fit at

the correct level, leaving a small clearance on each side (about ⅛″ (0.3 cm) all round).

18. Using the batten cut in step 9, cut three lengths of 10 ⅜″ (26.2 cm) and three lengths of 9 ½″ (24.1 cm). Set the sliding bevel against the angle on the inside of the vertical joints. On both floors set out the position of the three compartment divisions. On ⅜″ (1 cm) plywood, draw out the six divisions, taking the base dimensions from the floors and using the sliding bevel to set out the angled edge. Score across the grain and cut out the divisions. On the upper floor divisions, cut the corner notch to fit over the angled blocks glued to the inside of the cote. (The cote actually rests on these.)

19. Glue and screw a length of the angled batten to the vertical edge of each divisions, on the same face. Glue and pin the two sets of matching divisions together, and check that they fit correctly in to the cote. Glue and pin both to their respective floor. On the underside of the upper floor, glue three sets of short battens (3″ x 1″ x 1″ (7.6 cm x 2.5 cm x 2.5 cm)) to locate at the top edge of the lower divisions.

ROOF

20. Cut the six rafters from a piece of 3″ x ¾″ (7.6 cm x 1.9 cm) wood, to a length of 23″ (58.4 cm). Cut an angle of 45° at both ends.

21. Glue two pieces of 2″ x 1″ x 6″ (5.1 cm x 2.5 cm x 15.2 cm) wood together and trim the ends square. Draw an equal-sided hexagon at both ends and draw a line between the points on the face of the wood. Hold the piece in a vise and plane the beveled faces to the line.

22. Hold the center post in the vise and screw each rafter to it, countersinking the screw heads.

23. Stand the assembled rafters centrally on the cote, with each rafter sitting over a corner joint. Mark the point where the apexes of the corner joints touch the rafters. Mark out and cut a notch (bird's mouth) at this point on each rafter, to allow the roof to sit over the sides of the cote. Place the roof back on the cote and measure the distance from the cote sides to the end of the rafters (dimension a). Draw a line around the cote level with the bottom of the rafters (b).

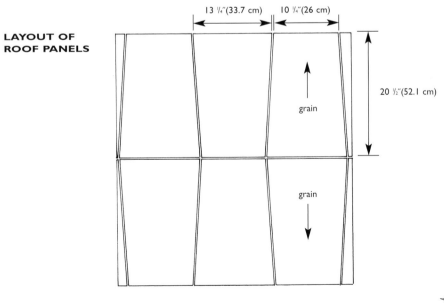

LAYOUT OF ROOF PANELS

13 ¼″(33.7 cm)   10 ¼″(26 cm)

20 ½″(52.1 cm)

grain

grain

Dovecote (continued)

SOFFIT BOARD

24. Cut six pieces of ⅜″(1 cm) plywood, 17″ (43.2 cm) long x (a + 1″ (2.5 cm)). Set the sliding bevel to 60° and transfer the angle to one end of each length of wood.

25. Cut the angle, on one end of each length. Measure the width of the cote side on the rafter line (b), and transfer this to each piece. Mark out and cut the opposite ends to the same angle. With the rafters sitting on the cote, check that the soffit boards touch the sides of the cote and that the miter faces meet. If any lengths are short, leaving the join open, lightly plane the back edge. Glue and pin the lengths to the rafters.

26. To allow the roof board to lie flat on the rafters, it is necessary to plane a bevel on either side of the top edge. Draw a center line down the edge of each rafter, and plane the bevel away to each side. Check the bevel between each pair of rafters by laying a straight edge across them. Plane the front top edge of the soffit board to lie flush with the beveled edges of the rafters and plane the front edge of each section of soffit board to an equal width, leaving a minimum of edge thickness of ¼″ (0.6 cm).

ROOF BOARDS

27. Cut six 18″ (45.7 cm) lengths of 4 ½″ x ⅜″ (11.4 cm x 1 cm) plywood. Set the sliding bevel to the angle between the front edge of the soffit board and the center line of the rafters. Transfer this angle to both a piece of scrap wood for future reference and to the end of one roof board. Measure the distance between the very top of the rafters and add 1″ (2.5 cm). Mark this length off along the front edge of the roof board. Mark out the end angle as before and cut the two angles.

28. Pin the board temporarily to the rafters, aligning the miter faces on the rafter center line, and the front edge parallel to the soffit board. Cut a second

board in the same way and lay it next to the first. The miter faces need to be slightly beveled for them to meet. Mark approximately half of the vertical angle on the edge of each board, and plane one miter face to it. Repeat this on the second face, lightly planing until the two faces meet. Set the sliding bevel to this angle and transfer it to a piece of scrap wood for future reference.

29. Glue and pin the bottom boards to the rafters before starting the next row. When cutting each of the remaining roof boards, mark both angles in a similar manner using the reference angles to mark out each board end, but cutting the angle in both directions in one cut. Slight adjustments can then be made by planing. Allow an overlap of at least ¾″ (1.9 cm) between each board, and plane a bevel on the top edge of each board as for the soffit board, to allow the next board to lie on a flat surface.

TOP VENT

30. Cut six tapered ¾″ (1.9 cm) blocks, 1 ½″ (3.8 cm) high at one end. Their length is taken from the remaining length of rafter after the roof boards are fitted. Before gluing the blocks in position it is necessary to remove the bevel from the rafters over this length. This can be done with a sharp chisel. Glue the blocks in place. Cut the center post ⅜″ (1 cm) higher than the vent blocks and plane a double bevel (as on the rafters) to run into the post.

31. Staple fine-gauge aluminum mesh over the front of the vent before cutting and fitting the final row of roof boards.

FINIALS

32. The top finial can be turned on a lathe, leaving a ¾″ (1.9 cm) spigot for gluing into a hole drilled in the center of the post. Alternatively, a turned wooden door knob can be used, screwed in place with a double-ended screw (handrail screw).

MOUNTING

33. Our dovecote was mounted on a 6″ (15.2 cm) square post. The top section was cut down to 4″ (10.2 cm) to locate in a metal cup (the type used for mounting fence posts on concrete or paving). The cup is bolted through the floor of the lower compartments. As a decorative feature, six false beams are screwed to the underside of the floor at each corner of the hexagon. Cut these—8 ½″ (21.6 cm) long—from 3″ x ¾″ (7.6 cm x 1.9 cm) wood. Draw the circular detail, and cut with the jigsaw.

FINISHING TOUCHES

34. After filling any defects and recessed pin and screw heads with epoxy filler, sand all surfaces smooth. The sides of the cote are primed and painted with a non-toxic paint system. The roof can be painted in a similar way, or sealed, primed, and finished with an exterior masonry paint.

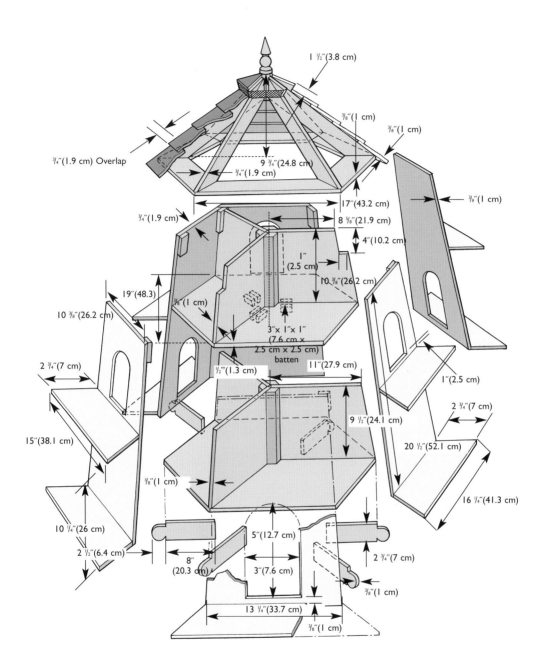

1 ½"(3.8 cm)

¾"(1.9 cm) Overlap

¾"(1.9 cm)

⅜"(1 cm)

⅜"(1 cm)

9 ¾"(24.8 cm)

¾"(1.9 cm)

17"(43.2 cm)

⅜"(1 cm)

¾"(1.9 cm)

8 ⅝"(21.9 cm)

4"(10.2 cm)

1"
(2.5 cm)

10 ⅜"(26.2 cm)

19"(48.3)

⅜"(1 cm)

10 ⅜"(26.2 cm)

3"x 1"x 1"
(7.6 cm x
2.5 cm x 2.5 cm)
batten

2 ¾"(7 cm)

½"(1.3 cm)

11"(27.9 cm)

9 ½"(24.1 cm)

1"(2.5 cm)

2 ¾"(7 cm)

15"(38.1 cm)

20 ½"(52.1 cm)

⅜"(1 cm)

16 ¼"(41.3 cm)

10 ¼"(26 cm)

2 ½"(6.4 cm)

5"(12.7 cm)

2 ¾"(7 cm)

8"
(20.3 cm)

3"(7.6 cm)

⅜"(1 cm)

13 ¼"(33.7 cm)

⅜"(1 cm)

Village House

1. Mark out the main parts and cut them roughly. Trim back to the pencil lines with a plane.

2. Draw parallel, horizontal lines in pencil and then cut shallow grooves in the wall pieces with a backsaw, using a scrap strip of wood as a guide, held in place with C-clamps.

3. To cut the main entry hole, clamp the front to the stand with a piece of scrap wood underneath and drill with a holesaw.

4. Glue and pin all the sides of the birdhouse together using a waterproof glue. Attach the roof, and glue and pin it into position.

5. Lay out the top section of the house and cut the sizes with a backsaw, trimming back to the lines with a plane. Cut the V-shaped section accurately with a backsaw.

6. Drill a smaller entry hole in this section, if required. Glue and pin to assemble.

7. Attach the smaller house on top of the large one. Glue and pin the top house to the lower one from the inside.

8. Using a fine-toothed saw, cut the dowel and the hardwood into the lengths given to make the balustrade. Use a ¼″ (0.6 cm) drill to make holes in the uprights to take the dowel.

9. Sand all parts of the house. Assemble the balustrade, gluing and then tapping the dowels into place.

10. Assemble all the parts of the house, using plated screws to withstand outdoor conditions.

11. Finish the outside by painting with water-based, exterior-grade undercoat, then a flat-finish top coat.

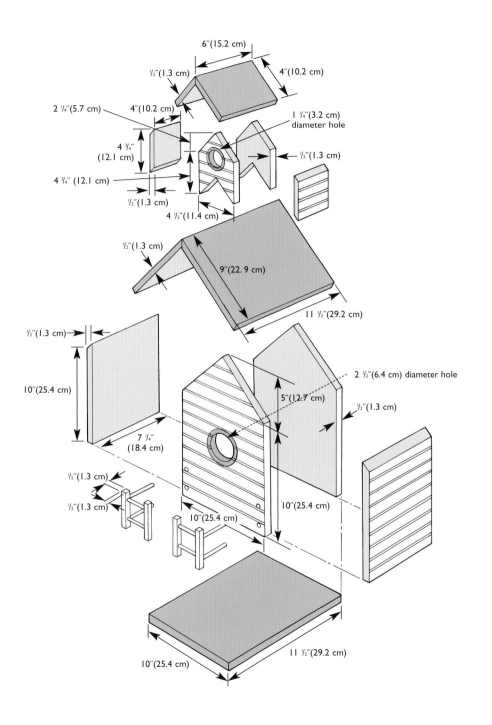

6″(15.2 cm)

½″(1.3 cm)

4″(10.2 cm)

2 ¼″(5.7 cm)

4″(10.2 cm)

1 ¼″(3.2 cm)
diameter hole

4 ¾″
(12.1 cm)

½″(1.3 cm)

4 ¾″ (12.1 cm)

½″(1.3 cm)

4 ½″(11.4 cm)

½″(1.3 cm)

9″(22. 9 cm)

11 ½″(29.2 cm)

½″(1.3 cm)

10″(25.4 cm)

2 ½″(6.4 cm) diameter hole

5″(12.7 cm)

½″(1.3 cm)

7 ¼″
(18.4 cm)

½″(1.3 cm)

½″(1.3 cm)

10″(25.4 cm)

10″(25.4 cm)

11 ½″(29.2 cm)

10″(25.4 cm)

Garden Shed

MATERIALS

39″ (99.1 cm) of 7″ × 11″ (17.8 cm × 27.9 cm) planed pine

12″ × 12″ (30.5 cm × 30.5 cm) square piece of 1/8″ (0.3 cm) exterior-grade plywood

12″ × 6″ (30.5 cm × 15.2 cm) piece of roofing felt

Brads

3/4″ (1.9 cm) nails

Scraps of wood

Yellow glue

Wood preservative

Black paint

Door security peephole

Sandpaper

TOOLS

Rule

Try square

Marking gauge

Backsaw

1″ (2.5 cm) chisel

Four 8″ (20.3 cm) C- or bar clamps

1″ (2.5 cm) and 1/2″ (1.3 cm) spade bits

Electric drill

Plane

Awl

Small hammer

Craft knife

Metal rule

1. Lay two 12″ (30.5 cm) lengths and two 6″ (15.2 cm) lengths on the pine, and cut these off with a backsaw.

2. Lay out and cut the slopes for the roof on the two smaller pieces, and trim to the line with a plane.

3. Using a marking gauge, lay rabbets on the long pieces.

4. Cut rabbets 8 1/2″ (21.6 cm) long x 7/8″ (2.2 cm) wide with a backsaw and if necessary trim the joint with a chisel. Make the step in the joint about 1/16″ (2 mm) more than the thickness of the wood.

5. With a metal ruler as a guide, and using an awl, mark a series of equally spaced parallel lines on the sides of the birdhouse.

6. Using the spade bit and electric drill, make a hole 1″ (2.5 cm) in diameter above the front door for the birds to enter and a hole to the side or rear to take your security peephole for viewing the birds.

7. Glue and assemble the four sides with the brads and clamp with the C- or bar clamps. Check with a try square to ensure the sides are at 90° before leaving the glue to set.

8. Plane the excess on the joint and the long sides to align with the slope for the roof.

9. Sand rough edges and surfaces with medium grade grit sandpaper.

10. Using a backsaw, cut three lengths of plywood: one piece 12″ × 6″ (30.5 cm x 15.2 cm) for the base; and two pieces 12″ × 3 1/8″ (30.5 cm x 8.4 cm) for the roof.

11. Glue and nail the plywood pieces to the birdhouse frame, and trim any excess with a plane.

12. Glue and nail the roofing felt to the plywood roof, and trim off any excess with a craft knife.

13. Cut scraps or a piece of thin molding into two pieces 4″ x 3/16″ (10.2 cm x .5 cm) and three pieces 2″ x 3/16″ (5.1 cm x .5 cm).

14. Glue all five pieces to the wall, making them into a window shape.

15. Give the sides and base a coating of wood preservative.

16. Lay out the door.

17. Paint the door and the window in black highlight their details.

18. Insert the peephole through both the wall of your shed and the birdhouse.

End panel (cut 2, 1 with entrance hole)

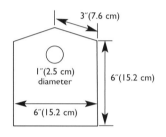

Side panel (cut 2)

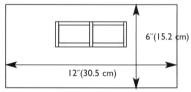

Roof (cut 2)

Base

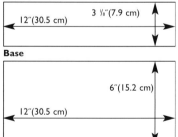

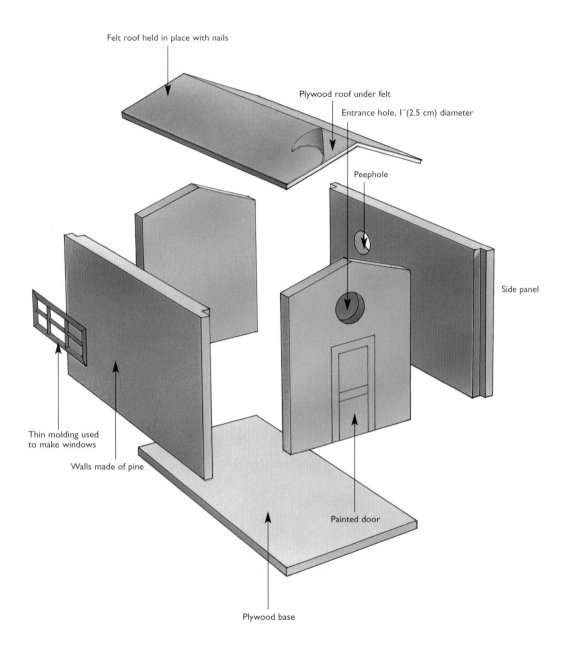

Felt roof held in place with nails

Plywood roof under felt

Entrance hole, 1″(2.5 cm) diameter

Peephole

Side panel

Thin molding used
to make windows

Walls made of pine

Painted door

Plywood base

Island Cottage

MATERIALS

40″ x 14″ (101.6 cm x 35.6 cm) piece of ⅝″ (1.6 cm) exterior grade MDF

32″ x 10″ (81.3 cm x 25.4 cm) piece of ⅛″ (0.3 cm) exterior grade plywood

6″ (15.2 cm) of 3″ x 2″ (7.6 cm x 5.1 cm) softwood

Brads

Yellow glue

Exterior grade primer, undercoat, and finishing paint

Sandpaper

TOOLS

Jigsaw

Plane

Sliding bevel

Electric drill

1 ¼″ (3.2 cm) spade bit

Backsaw

C-clamp

Hammer

Craft knife

Paintbrushes

Pencil

Steel rule

1. Following the template to the right, layout the back, sides, front, and base of the birdhouse on ⅝″ (1.6 cm) MDF. Cut out with a jigsaw and trim to pencil lines with a plane.

2. Set the sliding bevel to the slope of the roof. Using the set sliding bevel, lay out with the pencil the angle on front and back portions. Trim to line with a plane.

3. Mark the position on the front portion for the entrance hole and cut out, using the drill with a 1 ¼″ (3.2 cm) spade bit.

4. Using a pencil or knife, lay out parallel horizontal lines approximately ⅖″ (1 cm) apart on the four sides of the birdhouse. Then cut shallow grooves with a backsaw, using a scrap piece of wood held in place with C-clamps as a guide.

5. Assemble the base and sides of the birdhouse using yellow glue and 1 ¼″ (3.2 cm) brads.

6. Lay out and cut with a jigsaw two pieces of ⅛″ (0.3 cm) plywood for the roof and trim edges with a plane.

7. On a 65″ (15.2 cm) length of 2″ x 3″ (5.1 cm x 7.6 cm) softwood—finished size 1 ¾″–2 ¼″ (4.4 cm x 5.7 cm)—lay out on either end the front shape of dormer window. Remove excess wood with a plane.

8. Using the already set sliding bevel, lay out roof angle and cut dormer with backsaw.

9. Glue and nail the dormer windows to one of the roof slopes, using ⅝″ (1.6 cm) brads.

10. Glue and nail the roof into position.

11. On remaining plywood, lay out a rectangle for the door, squares for windows, and strips for a picket fence. Cut out with a backsaw and sand the edges with medium grade grit sandpaper to remove all saw marks.

12. With a craft knife and a steel rule, cut vertical lines on the door to achieve a boarded effect.

13. Using medium grade grit sandpaper, thoroughly sand birdhouse and then glue on door, windows, and picket fence.

14. Apply one coat of primer paint, allow to dry, sand with fine grade grit sandpaper, and then apply undercoat.

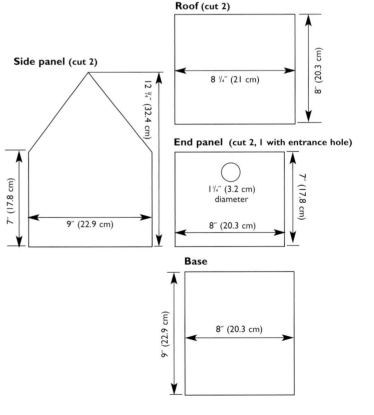

Side panel (cut 2)

12 ¾″ (32.4 cm)

7″ (17.8 cm)

9″ (22.9 cm)

Roof (cut 2)

8 ¼″ (21 cm)

8″ (20.3 cm)

End panel (cut 2, 1 with entrance hole)

1 ¼″ (3.2 cm) diameter

8″ (20.3 cm)

7″ (17.8 cm)

Base

9″ (22.9 cm)

8″ (20.3 cm)

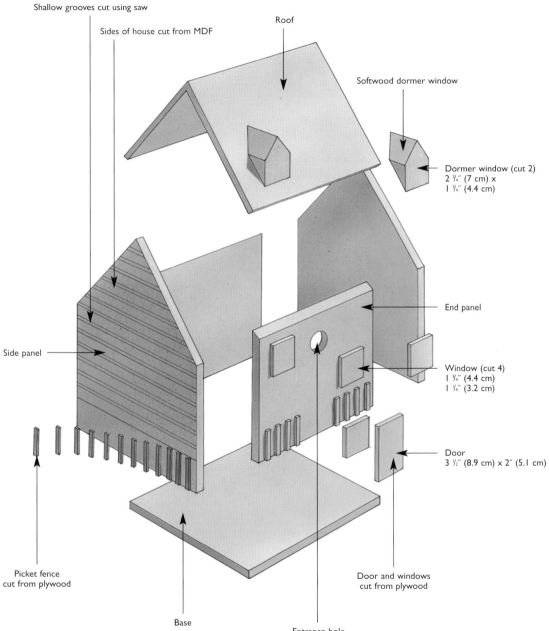

Shallow grooves cut using saw

Sides of house cut from MDF

Roof

Softwood dormer window

Dormer window (cut 2)
2 ³/₄″ (7 cm) x
1 ³/₄″ (4.4 cm)

End panel

Side panel

Window (cut 4)
1 ³/₄″ (4.4 cm)
1 ¼″ (3.2 cm)

Door
3 ½″ (8.9 cm) x 2″ (5.1 cm)

Picket fence
cut from plywood

Door and windows
cut from plywood

Base

Entrance hole
1 ¼″ (3.2 cm) diameter

Calvary House

MATERIALS

40″ x 20″ (101.6 cm x 50.8 cm) piece of ⅝″ (1.6 cm) exterior grade MDF

40″ x 20″ (101.6 cm x 50.8 cm) piece of ⅛″ (0.3 cm) exterior grade plywood

4′ x ½″ (1.2 m x 1.3 cm) length of hardwood dowel

Length 2″ x 2″ (5.1 cm x 5.1 cm) planed softwood

4″ (10.2 cm) scrap of softwood, finished section ⅞″ x 1 ¼″ (2.2 cm x 3.2 cm)

Sandpaper

Exterior wood stain/preservative

Yellow glue

Brads

Two No. 10 3″ (7.6 cm) countersunk plated woodscrews

Plastic film canister

TOOLS

Jigsaw

Electric drill

½″ (1.3 cm) twist drill bit

1 ¼″ (3.2 cm) spade bit

Miter square or sliding bevel

Hammer

Backsaw

Chisel

Mallet

Paintbrushes

Screwdriver

Plane

1. Lay out, then use a jigsaw to cut two pieces of ⅝″ (1.6 cm) MDF for the platform and the eaves. Trim down to the line with a plane. For dimensions, see the template to the right and on page 149.

2. Lay out eight points on the platform, 1 ¼″ (3.2 cm) from the edge. Place the eaves board on top of the platform and drill eight ½″ (1.3 cm) holes through both pieces.

3. With a plane, bevel the edge of the eaves board all around to an angle of 45°. Test for accuracy with a miter square or sliding bevel set at 45°.

4. Using the electric drill fitted with a 1 ¼″ (3.2 cm) spade bit, make a hole in the platform for a water trough (plastic film canister).

5. Cut three pieces of ⅛″ (0.3 cm) plywood for the door and windows: glue and nail these to one side of the 10″ x 4″ x 4″ (25.4 cm x 10.2 cm x 10.2 cm) softwood.

6. Cut eight lengths of ½″ (1.3 cm) dowel to a length of 5 ⅛″ (13 cm) with a backsaw. Attach the piece of softwood block to the platform with yellow glue and brads.

7. Glue and assemble the eight lengths of dowel with the platform and the eaves. When the glue has set, use a plane to trim off the excess dowel that protrudes through the eaves.

8. Cut two roof supports and a base support out of the remaining MDF, using a jigsaw. Finish the edges with a plane.

9. Cut out ⅛″ (.3 cm) plywood for the roof; glue and nail in conjunction with the roof supports. Trim off any excess plywood with a plane. Cut two pieces of softwood for chimneys, 1 ¾″ x 1 ¼″ x ⅞″ (4.4 cm x 3.2 cm x 2.2 cm); cut out 45° V-shapes and glue to roof. Use beading to give the roof a log effect.

10. Lay out and cut a vertical slot 4″ (10.2 cm) deep and 5.8″ (1.6 cm) in the base support/stand. Cut vertically with a backsaw and chop out the central section with a ⅝″ (1.6 cm) chisel. Spread glue in the slot and insert the base support.

11. When the glue on the base support/stand has set, drill two ⁷⁄₁₆″ (0.5 cm) holes in it and screw it to the underside of the platform.

12. Sand down with medium grade grit sandpaper, then apply two coats of wood

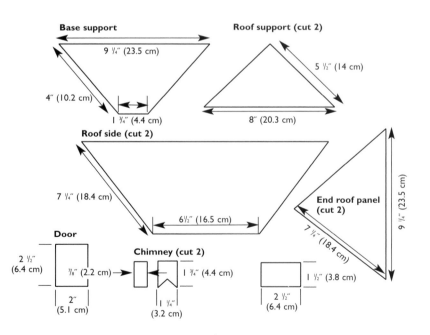

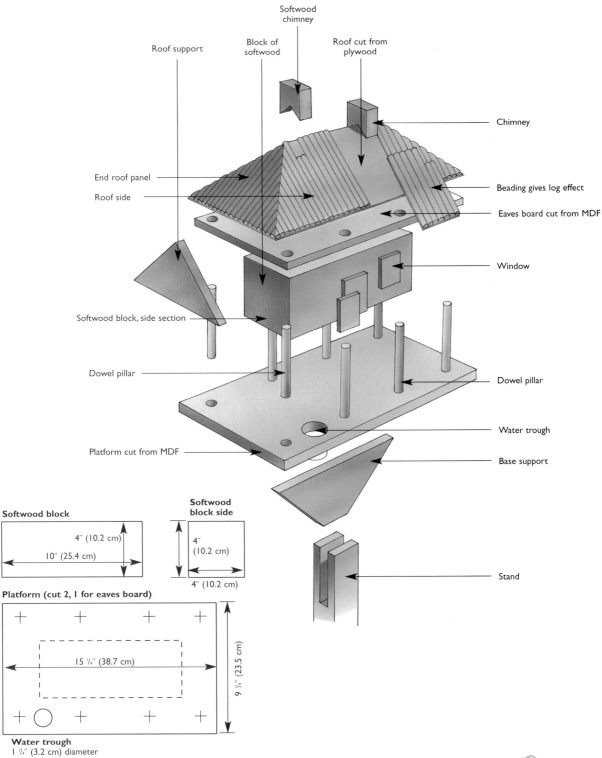

Softwood
chimney

Block of
softwood

Roof cut from
plywood

Roof support

Chimney

End roof panel

Beading gives log effect

Roof side

Eaves board cut from MDF

Window

Softwood block, side section

Dowel pillar

Dowel pillar

Water trough

Platform cut from MDF

Base support

Softwood block

4" (10.2 cm)

10" (25.4 cm)

**Softwood
block side**

4"
(10.2 cm)

4" (10.2 cm)

Stand

Platform (cut 2, 1 for eaves board)

15 ¼" (38.7 cm)

9 ¼" (23.5 cm)

Water trough
1 ¼" (3.2 cm) diameter

Birdhouse Plans **149**

Villa

1. Following the template below and right, lay out pieces for the base and portico roof from ¾″ (1.9 cm) MDF; the sides, front, back, and roof from ½″ (1.3 cm) MDF; the portico steps, window, and door from ¼″ (0.6 cm) MDF; the portico pillars 3 ½″ (8.9 cm) from ⅝″ (1.6 cm) dowel. Cut the MDF pretty close to the lines with a jigsaw and trim down to exact size with a plane. Cut the hardwood dowel with a backsaw.

2. Lay out the center of the front portico of the birdhouse; with an electric drill, fitted with a 1 ¼″ (3.2 cm) spade bit, drill a hole.

3. Chamfer three edges of the base with a plane.

4. Assemble all sides and roof by gluing and nailing together.

5. In the center of the front roof peak drill a blind hole (on that does not go right through) with a ¾″ (1.9 cm) auger bit fitted to a brace. (An electric drill can be very difficult to control and might pull straight through.)

6. Thoroughly sand the birdhouse and the edges of the steps, door, and window with medium grade grit sandpaper.

7. From the remaining ¼″ (0.6 cm) plywood, cut eight strips ¾″ x 12″ (1.9 cm x 30.5 cm) using a jigsaw fitted with a fine blade; trim to precise size with a plane.

8. With a pencil, mark steps at 1 ⅛″ (2.9 cm) intervals to a depth of ⅜″ (1 cm) (halfway); make cuts with a backsaw and chop out with a 1″ (2.5 cm) chisel and mallet. Use a coarse file to smooth out any irregularities in the steps.

9. Apply glue and attach this plywood to the corners of the birdhouse with a heavy-duty staple gun or brads.

10. Apply glue to the door and windows and staple or nail them into position.

11. Assemble the portico by gluing and nailing the steps into the dowel end from underneath, and also from the top.

12. Glue and nail the portico into position around the door.

13. Cut roofing felt with a craft knife and staple or nail it to the roof.

14. Apply primer paint, undercoat, and the finishing color to the birdhouse, lightly sanding down between each coat with fine sandpaper.

15. Highlight window detail by painting in black with a No. 6 artist's brush.

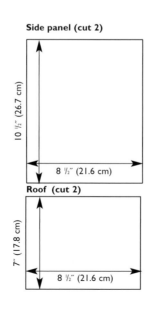

Side panel (cut 2)

10 ½″ (26.7 cm)

8 ½″ (21.6 cm)

Roof (cut 2)

7″ (17.8 cm)

8 ½″ (21.6 cm)

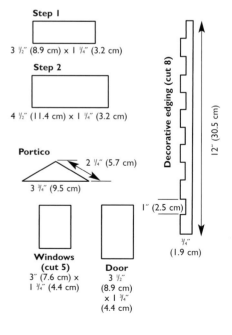

Step 1

3 ½″ (8.9 cm) x 1 ¼″ (3.2 cm)

Step 2

4 ½″ (11.4 cm) x 1 ¼″ (3.2 cm)

Portico

2 ¼″ (5.7 cm)

3 ¾″ (9.5 cm)

Windows (cut 5)
3″ (7.6 cm) x 1 ¾″ (4.4 cm)

Door
3 ½″ (8.9 cm) x 1 ¾″ (4.4 cm)

Decorative edging (cut 8)

12″ (30.5 cm)

1″ (2.5 cm)

¾″ (1.9 cm)

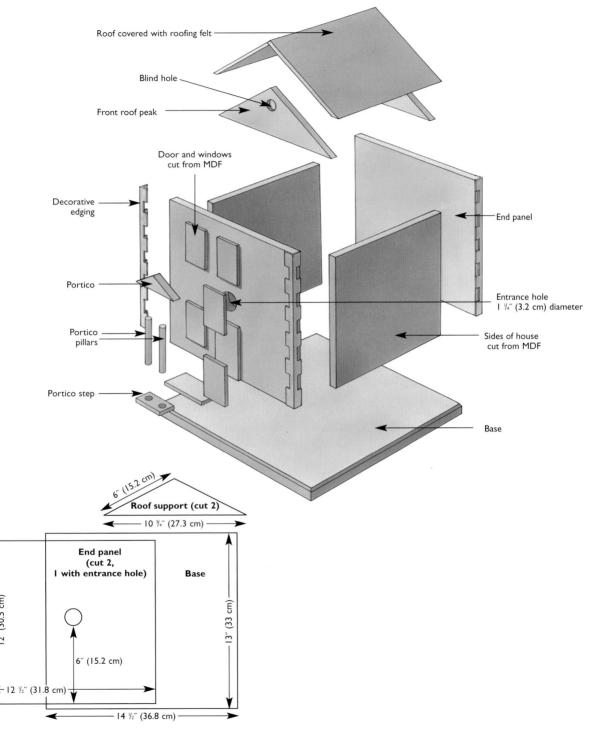

Roof covered with roofing felt

Blind hole

Front roof peak

Door and windows
cut from MDF

Decorative
edging

End panel

Portico

Entrance hole
1 ¼" (3.2 cm) diameter

Portico
pillars

Sides of house
cut from MDF

Portico step

Base

6" (15.2 cm)

Roof support (cut 2)

10 ¾" (27.3 cm)

12" (30.5 cm)

**End panel
(cut 2,
1 with entrance hole)**

Base

13" (33 cm)

6" (15.2 cm)

12 ½" (31.8 cm)

14 ½" (36.8 cm)

Birdhouse Plans

Mexican Mission

MATERIALS

30" (76.2 cm) square piece of No. 5 ⅝" (1.6 cm) exterior grade plywood

20" (50.8 cm) length of ⅜" (1 cm) diameter hardwood dowel

Brads

Brass eyelet and hook

Scraps of softwood

Sand

Yellow glue

Exterior paint

Sandpaper

TOOLS

Panel or circular saw

Drill

⅜" (1 cm) auger bit

Fretsaw or jigsaw

Hammer

Tape measure

Try square

1. Cut front, back, sides, base, and roof out of the plywood following the template below and right. Use a panel saw for the straight edges and a fretsaw or jigsaw for the stepped tops of the front and back.

2. Clean up all the rough edges with medium grade grit sandpaper.

3. Lay out the measurements for the 11" x 1 ½" (27.9 cm x 3.8 cm) slit opening on one side. Make a starter hole in one corner for the marked area with a drill bit.

4. Clamp a straight piece of plywood to the side to act as a guide, and cut the slit opening using a jigsaw.

5. Drill 12 holes in the base for drainage.

6. Mark positions for the dowels along both sides.

7. Place scrap plywood under the sides and drill the holes for the dowels.

8. Lay out the measurements of the bell recess on the plywood following the template.

9. Make a starter hole as in step 3 in one corner of the laid out bell and cut out the shape with a jigsaw.

10. Cut out the plywood dummy side windows, the front windows, and the arched door to the measurements on the template.

11. Glue and nail the windows and door into place, making sure they are symmetrical.

12. Assemble the church using brads, and apply yellow glue along all meeting edges.

13. Smooth the top of the visible plywood with sandpaper to level all the top edges.

14. Cut twelve 1 ¼" (3.2 cm) long pieces of ⅛" (0.3 cm) dowel.

15. Tap one 1 ¼" (4.4 cm) section of dowel into each side hole. These make the roof beams.

16. Cut out the small plywood cross with a fretsaw or jigsaw following the template shape traced on the wood.

17. Cut off the head of a brad, and use both ends of the brad to attach the cross to the top of the back wall.

18. Shape a bell from a piece of softwood, following the template. Alternatively, turn it on a lathe.

19. Attach the bell to the front of the church with the brass eyelet and hook.

20. Coat the sides and top with a diluted yellow glue solution and, before it is anywhere near dry, sprinkle sand evenly over the surface.

21. Brush wood preservative onto the base of the box.

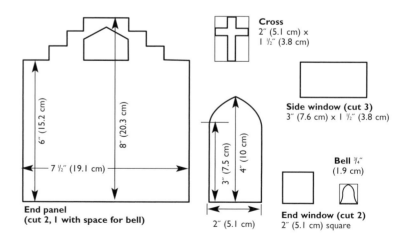

End panel
(cut 2, 1 with space for bell)

6" (15.2 cm)   8" (20.3 cm)   7 ½" (19.1 cm)

3" (7.5 cm)   4" (10 cm)   2" (5.1 cm)

Cross
2" (5.1 cm) x
1 ½" (3.8 cm)

Side window (cut 3)
3" (7.6 cm) x 1 ½" (3.8 cm)

Bell ¾"
(1.9 cm)

End window (cut 2)
2" (5.1 cm) square

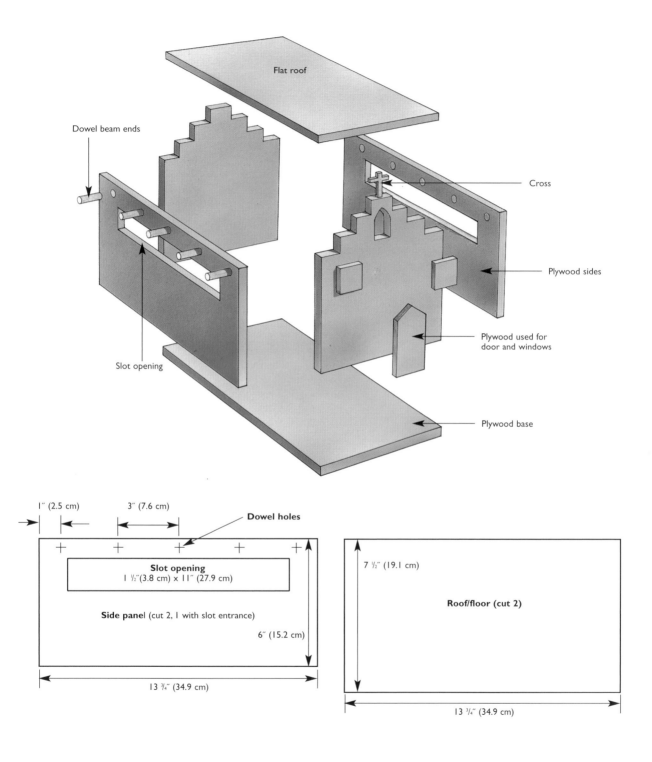

Flat roof

Dowel beam ends

Cross

Slot opening

Plywood sides

Plywood used for door and windows

Plywood base

1″ (2.5 cm) 3″ (7.6 cm)

Dowel holes

Slot opening
1 ½″(3.8 cm) x 11″ (27.9 cm)

Side panel (cut 2, 1 with slot entrance)

6″ (15.2 cm)

13 ¾″ (34.9 cm)

7 ½″ (19.1 cm)

Roof/floor (cut 2)

13 ¾″ (34.9 cm)

Thatched-roof Cottage

MATERIALS

4′ (121.9 cm) square piece of ¼″ (0.6 cm) exterior grade MDF

Pieces of ⅜″ (1 cm) exterior grade MDF, approx. 5″ x 10″ (12.7 cm x 25.4 cm)

Strips of ⅜″ (1 cm) square hardwood, plus 4″ x 3″ (10.2 cm x 7.6 cm) rectangle for door

Roofing felt

Yellow glue

Exterior paint

Brads

Sandpaper

TOOLS

Jigsaw

Electric drill

Hammer

Craft knife

Try square

Tape measure and pencil

Hand plane

Paintbrushes

1. Following the template at right, lay out all the components of the house on the sheet of MDF, being careful to make the sides parallel with a try square. Lay out the two sides of the porch on the scrap of thicker MDF.

2. Cut out each part, remembering to cut out the opening between the porch and the main structure on the front section if you wish to attract larger birds. Drill entrance hole in front section of the porch.

3. Nail and glue the bottom, sides, and front of the house together and set aside to dry. Check that the corners are at 90° with the try square.

4. Chamfer the top edges of the front and back of the building and the top edges of the porch sides.

5. Attach the porch sides to the front wall with yellow glue and two brads per side.

6. Glue and nail the front of the porch in place before painting the exterior of the house in your chosen color. This should be a neutral tone to mimic wattle and daub, or flat white.

7. Attach the roof sections of the porch and main house in the same way. One edge overlaps the other at the apex to form a neat joint.

8. Nail on the thin roofing felt and trim the edges to give an exact fit over the MDF pieces of roof. Space the brads at approximately 1″ (2.5 cm) intervals.

9. The last stage of the structure is to nail and glue small pieces of the hardwood molding around the walls to represent beams. Use a craft knife to chamfer the outside edges of the molding before cutting it to the required length. Add a thin section for the front door.

10. Paint the beams flat black and paint on more decorative detail, such as windows, with a small artist's brush.

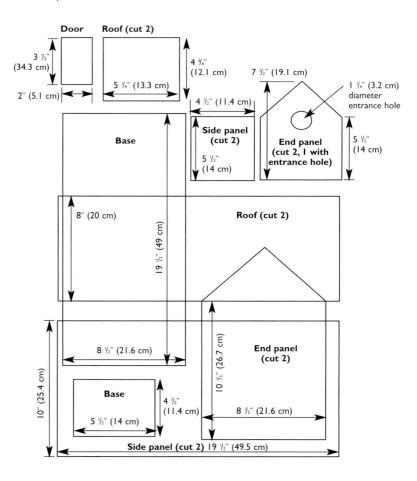

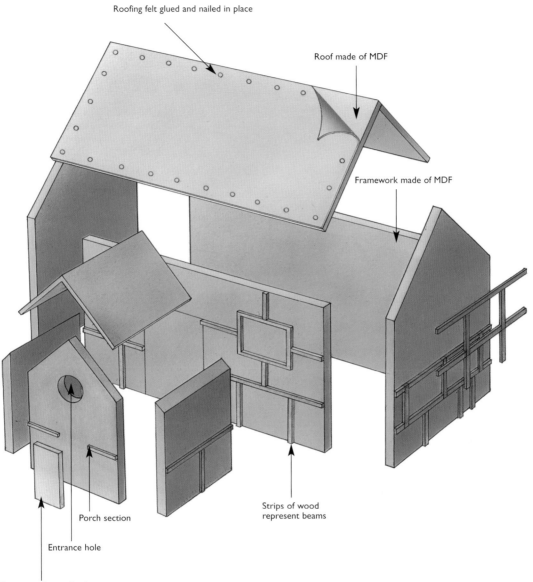

Roofing felt glued and nailed in place

Roof made of MDF

Framework made of MDF

Strips of wood
represent beams

Porch section

Entrance hole

Scraps used to make door

Plantation House

1. On the ¾″ (1.9 cm) MDF lay out the base 14″ x 7 ½″ (35.6 cm x 19.1 cm), the bottom 11 ½″ x 5 ⅛″ (29.2 cm x 13 cm), two sides 11 ½″ x 5 ⅛″ (29.2 cm x 13 cm), and two ends 5 ⅛″ x 7 ⅝″ (13 cm x 19.4 cm) of the birdhouse. (Layout the two ends so that the peak forms at a 90° angle.) Cut slightly oversize with a jigsaw and trim to lines with a plane.

2. Use a plane to chamfer three edges of the base, and sand smooth.

3. Glue and nail all these pieces together.

4. When the glue has set, trim off any irregularities with a plane.

5. Lay out and cut two piece of ¼″ (0.6 cm) MDF for the roof, trim to 4 ⅜″ x 12 ¼″ (11 cm x 31.1 cm) with a plane and then glue and nail these to the main body of the birdhouse.

6. On the ¼″ (0.6 cm) MDF lay out the four small squares 1 ⅜″ x 1 ⅜″ (3.4 cm x 3.4 cm) for the pillar bases and tops. Cut with a backsaw and then smooth off the edges with medium grade grit sandpaper. Draw diagonal lines to find the center and make an indentation with an awl.

7. With a backsaw and a bracing board, cut two piece of ⅞″ (2.2 cm) dowel 4 ½″ (11.4 cm) long. Then glue and nail the pillar bases to the dowel.

8. Chamfer the pillar bases and tops with a chisel.

9. From the remaining ¼″ (0.6 cm) MDF cut a piece for the door 2″ x 3 ⅛″ (5.1 cm x 7.9 cm) and four ¾″ x 2 ¾″ (1.9 cm x 7 cm) pieces for the window. Glue and nail the door into position but leave the windows.

10. From a scrap of ¾″ (1.9 cm) MDF, cut a triangle 4″ x 5 ⅛″ (10.2 cm x 13 cm) from the top of the portico. Sand the edges; mark the middle and make a hole with the electric drill fitted with a 1 ¼″ (3.2 cm) spade bit. Tidy up the inside of the hole with sandpaper. Sand any marks left by the spade bit.

11. Assemble the portico by gluing and nailing.

12. Mark and cut two angled pieces of ¼″ (0.6 cm) MDF for the portico roof 3 ⅜″ x 4″ (8.4 cm x 10.2 cm); glue and nail these into position.

13. Glue and nail windows into position.

14. From the two pieces of softwood, cut the wood for the spires; two 3 ½″ (8.9 cm) long from the thinner piece and one 5″ (12.7 cm) long from the thicker. Mark out 90° V-shapes on them and cut away with a backsaw, so that they sit precisely on top of the roof. With a pencil, mark in ¼″ (0.6 cm) halfway up the spires and reduce the width with the backsaw to create a stepped effect.

15. Mark lines for a pyramid point, cut with backsaw, and glue and nail these to the roof.

16. Using a medium grade grit sandpaper, remove any saw marks.

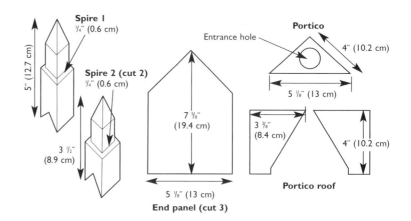

Spire 1
¼″ (0.6 cm)

5″ (12.7 cm)

Spire 2 (cut 2)
¼″ (0.6 cm)

3 ½″
(8.9 cm)

Entrance hole

7 ⅝″
(19.4 cm)

5 ⅛″ (13 cm)

End panel (cut 3)

Portico

4″ (10.2 cm)

5 ⅛″ (13 cm)

3 ⅜″
(8.4 cm)

4″ (10.2 cm)

Portico roof

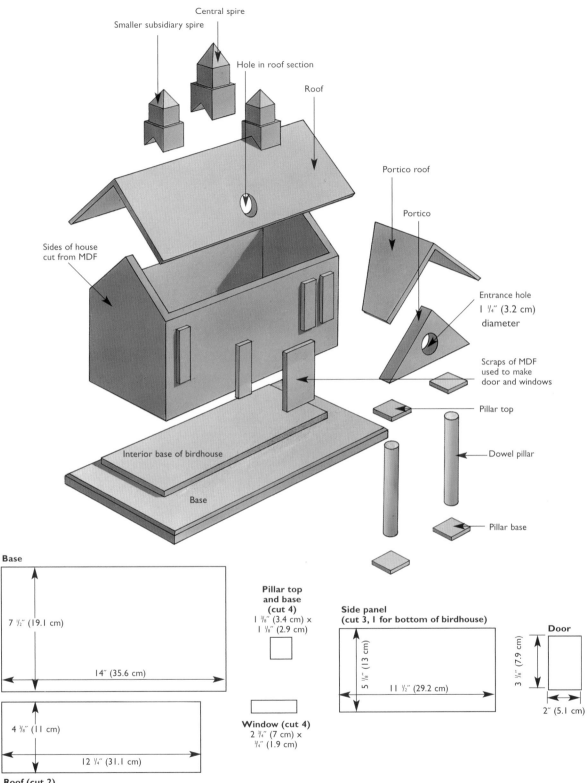

Smaller subsidiary spire

Central spire

Hole in roof section

Roof

Portico roof

Portico

Sides of house
cut from MDF

Entrance hole
1 ¼" (3.2 cm)
diameter

Scraps of MDF
used to make
door and windows

Pillar top

Interior base of birdhouse

Dowel pillar

Base

Pillar base

Base

7 ½" (19.1 cm)

14" (35.6 cm)

**Pillar top
and base
(cut 4)**
1 ⅜" (3.4 cm) ×
1 ⅛" (2.9 cm)

**Side panel
(cut 3, 1 for bottom of birdhouse)**

5 ⅛" (13 cm)

11 ½" (29.2 cm)

Door

3 ⅛" (7.9 cm)

2" (5.1 cm)

4 ⅜" (11 cm)

12 ¼" (31.1 cm)

Roof (cut 2)

Window (cut 4)
2 ¾" (7 cm) ×
¾" (1.9 cm)

Birdhouse Plans

Windmill Nest Box

MATERIALS

Quarter panel 24″ x 48″ (61 cm x 121.9 cm) No. 6 ⅜″ (1 cm) exterior grade plywood

One-eighth panel 24″ (61 cm) square No. 4 ¼″ (.6 cm) exterior grade plywood

6″ x 6″ x 1″ (15.2 cm x 15.2 cm x 2.5 cm) piece of pine

4″ (10.2 cm) length of ¼″ (0.6 cm) dowel

Plastic lid to fit grooved hole 3″ (7.6 cm) diameter

3 ⅛″ x 4″ (7.9 cm x 10.2 cm) piece of galvanized wire mesh

Bowl to fit in hole 3 ½″ (8.9 cm) diameter

Four No. 6 ¾″ (17.1 cm) countersunk plated wood screws

Brads

Staples

2″ (5.1 cm) plated flush hinge and No. 4 ½″ (1.3 cm) screws

Yellow glue

Sandpaper

¾″ (1.9 cm) long piece of 1″ (2.5 cm) dowel (or old broom handle) for the spacer

One No. 10 2″ (5.1 cm) japanned round head screw

6″ (15.2 cm) square piece of roofing lead

Exterior primer

Exterior paint

TOOLS

Jigsaw

Plane

Pair of compasses

Sliding bevel

Electric drill and bit

Craft knife

Awl

Screwdriver

Coarse rasp or plane

Metal snips

Paintbrushes

Metal ruler

1. Following the template at right or by using a pair of compasses, lay out three circles on ⅜″ (1 cm) plywood to the following measurements: two 4 ¾″ (12.1 cm) in diameter for top and second floor; one 9 ¾″ (24.8 cm) in diameter for the ground floor; and one 20″ (61 cm) in diameter for the base.

2. Once the circle is measured, use the radius to mark off each side of the hexagon. Cut out each hexagon with a jigsaw, and trim each to line with a plane.

3. On the base hexagon, use a pair of compasses to lay out a circle that is slightly smaller in diameter than the drinking bowl. The circle in our model is 3 ½″ (8.9 cm) in diameter. Drill a starter hole inside the circle and cut out with a jigsaw.

4. Lay and cut out a circular hole in the second floor for the plastic feeding tray following the instructions in step 3. The plastic lid in our model fits a hold 3″ (7.6 cm) in diameter.

5. Lay out six side pieces on ⅜″ (1 cm) plywood to the following measurements: 24″ (61 cm) tall, 4 ½″ (11.4 cm) at the base, and 2 ½″ (6.4 cm) at the top.

6. Set your sliding bevel to 60° and, with a pencil, mark the angles on the top and the bottom of the side pieces, and then trim them to the angle with a plane.

7. Glue and nail two sides to the ground floor and the first floor.

8. While the glue is setting, lay out the window and door on ⅜″ (1 cm) plywood and cut these out with a jigsaw.

9. Attach wire mesh to the inside of the window using staples. Optional: to attach the mesh flush to the outside of the window, cut it into shape and attach it with staples (you may need very fine mesh to shape it accurately); alternatively, to shape the mesh, bend it around the inside of the window, and fasten it from the back.

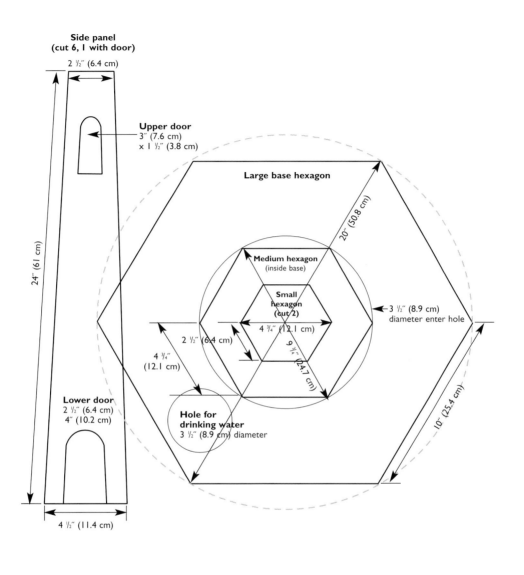

**Side panel
(cut 6, 1 with door)**

2 ½" (6.4 cm)

Upper door
3" (7.6 cm)
x 1 ½" (3.8 cm)

24" (61 cm)

Large base hexagon

20" (50.8 cm)

Medium hexagon
(inside base)

**Small
hexagon
(cut 2)**

4 ¾" (12.1 cm)

2 ½" (6.4 cm)

3 ½" (8.9 cm)
diameter enter hole

9 ¾" (24.7 cm)

4 ¾"
(12.1 cm)

10" (25.4 cm)

Lower door
2 ½" (6.4 cm)
4" (10.2 cm)

**Hole for
drinking water**
3 ½" (8.9 cm) diameter

4 ½" (11.4 cm)

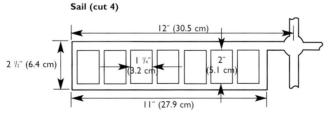

Sail (cut 4)

12" (30.5 cm)

2 ½" (6.4 cm)

1 ¼"
(3.2 cm)

2"
(5.1 cm)

11" (27.9 cm)

Windmill Nest Box (continued)

10. Glue and nail the remaining sides one at a time to the ground floor and second floor and to each other. Hold the tops together with a staple. A rubber band or masking tape are useful clamping aids.

11. When all the glue has set, smooth down the whole work using sandpaper.

12. Using an awl and a metal rule as a guide, score parallel lines on all sides to achieve a wood-clad effect.

13. Smooth the base hexagon.

14. Attach the base to the underside of the birdhouse with four No. 4 ³/₄″ (1.9 cm) countersunk plated wood screws.

15. Lay out a 2 ¹/₂″ (6.4 cm) diameter hexagon on the pine for the roof.

16. Cut out the roof with a jigsaw and round off the top edge with a coarse rasp of a plane.

17. Cut the lead into a rough circle 3 ¹/₄″ (8.3 cm) in diameter with metal snips.

18. Hammer the lead into the shape of the roof. This is best done gradually, by working your way around the shape.

19. When the lead roof is completely formed, cut off the excess and secure the lead to the roof with brads.

20. Attach the 2″ (5.1 cm) plated flush hinge to the roof with the No. 4 ¹/₂″ (1.3 cm) screws.

21. Drill two holes ¹/₄″ (0.6 cm) in diameter under the window.

22. Put a drop of glue in the holes and insert one 2″ (5.1 cm) length of ¹/₄″ (0.6 cm) dowel into each hole.

23. Using the template, draw the silhouette of the wind vanes (sails) on the veneer core plywood. Mark the outline precisely with a craft knife.

24. Cut out the vanes with a jigsaw fitted with a fine blade. If necessary, finish off the edges with a coarse file.

25. Drill a hole in the center of the vanes and in the center of the 1″ (2.5 cm) spacer.

26. Attach the vanes and the spacer to the center of the front side of the birdhouse with a No. 10 2″ (5.1 cm) coated round head screw.

27. Finish the birdhouse by painting with exterior grade gloss.

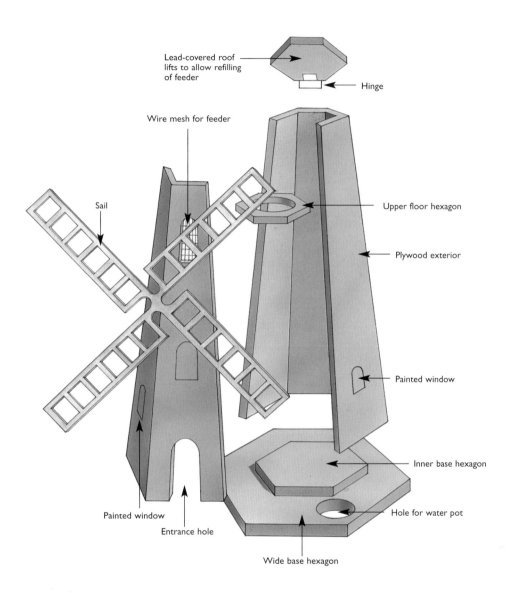

Lead-covered roof lifts to allow refilling of feeder

Hinge

Wire mesh for feeder

Sail

Upper floor hexagon

Plywood exterior

Painted window

Inner base hexagon

Painted window

Entrance hole

Hole for water pot

Wide base hexagon

Renaissance Romance

MATERIALS

48″ x 24″ (121.9 cm x 61 cm) sheet of ⅜″ (1 cm) exterior grade MDF

Approximately 15″ x 12″ (38.1 cm x 30.5 cm) piece of ¾″ (1.9 cm) exterior grade MDF

Scraps of black plastic sheeting or plywood that has been painted black

Block of softwood, approximately 5″ x 5″ x 5″ (12.7 cm x 12.7 cm x 12.7 cm)

Black and gray eggshell paint

Brads

Yellow glue

Sandpaper

TOOLS

Jigsaw or fretsaw

Electric drill and drill bit

Panel saw or circular saw

Backsaw

Plane

Stapler

Try square

Tape measure

Pencil

Paintbrushes

1. Following the template at right, lay out the castle sections on the ⅜″ (1 cm) MDF sheet and cut out with a panel saw or circular saw. Sand smooth any rough-cut edges.

2. Do the same with the ¾″ (1.9 cm) MDF that will be used as the base.

3. Next, mark the positions of the arched window shapes on the front of the castle and tower. These are 2 ¾″ (7 cm) high and 1 ¼″ (3.2 cm) wide on the house and 1 ½″ (3.8 cm) high by ¾″ (1.9 cm) wide on the tower. Use a poster board template to make sure that the windows are all the same shape.

4. Cut out the windows with a jigsaw or fretsaw. Use a drill and drill bit to make pilot holes for each window. The circular

1 ¼″ (3.2 cm) diameter entrance hole at the side of the tower should also be cut out at this stage. This is 7″ (17.8 cm) above the level of the base.

5. To give the appearance of weatherboard cladding, use a backsaw guided by a straightedge to make shallow cuts at ⅝″ (1.6 cm) intervals horizontally across the walls.

6. Paint the front of the tower and castle with the eggshell paint, giving the birdhouse a distressed gray appearance. Painting these sections at this stage means that the inside edges of the window can be coated before the inner plastic sheet is added.

7. Staple a section of the back plastic sheeting to the back of the window areas. The piece on the inside of the tower should be 2″ (5.1 cm) wide and about 7″ (17.8 cm) long. The larger piece needed to blacken the castle windows should be cut 9″ (22.9 cm) wide and 7″ (17.8 cm) high. Plywood could be used as an alternative to plastic.

8. Assemble the walls of the castle on the base using brads and glue.

9. Add the tower, again with brads and glue. Nail a square block of scrap MDF at

the base of the tower to hold each of the walls square at the base.

10. After painting the rest of the walls, add the two 7″ x 8 ½″ (17.8 cm x 21.6 cm) roof sections, nailing and gluing them in place. The MDF sections overlap at the apex and the left-hand piece is shaped to fit around the tower at its edge.

11. The make the top of the tower, plane the softwood block to make a steeply sloping roof. The finished height is 4 ½″ (11.4 cm) and the top should be 3″ (7.6 cm) wide and 2″ (5.1 cm) deep.

12. Smooth the wood with sandpaper and center the roof on the top of the tower, attaching with yellow glue.

13. Cut out the shaped 7″ (17.8 cm) long trim with a jigsaw or fretsaw and attach to the front of the roof with brads and glue. You can easily vary the pattern of the trim, but the finished width should be around ¾″ (1.9 cm) wide.

14. Finally, cut out the 3 ½″ (8.9 cm) wide and 4 ¼″ (10.8 cm) high door shape from a scrap of the ⅜″ (1 cm) MDF and glue it to the front of the birdhouse.

15. Coat all the remaining sections with the eggshell paint.

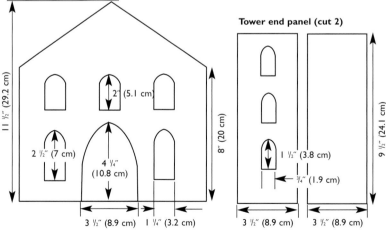

End panel (cut 2)

11 ½″ (29.2 cm)

2″ (5.1 cm)

2 ½″ (7 cm)

4 ¼″ (10.8 cm)

8″ (20 cm)

3 ½″ (8.9 cm)   1 ¼″ (3.2 cm)

Tower end panel (cut 2)

1 ½″ (3.8 cm)

¾″ (1.9 cm)

9 ½″ (24.1 cm)

3 ½″ (8.9 cm)   3 ½″ (8.9 cm)

  The New Birdhouse Book

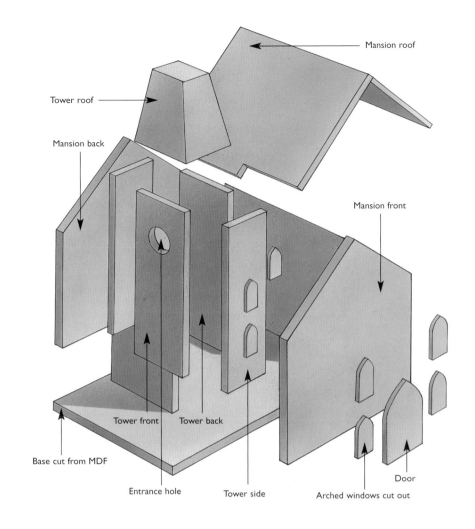

Mansion roof

Tower roof

Mansion back

Mansion front

Tower front   Tower back

Base cut from MDF

Entrance hole   Tower side

Door

Arched windows cut out

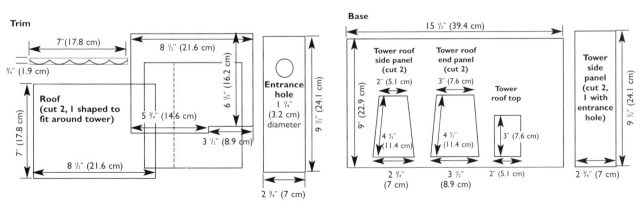

Trim

7"(17.8 cm)

¾" (1.9 cm)

7" (17.8 cm)

8 ½" (21.6 cm)

6 ½" (16.2 cm)

Roof
(cut 2, 1 shaped to
fit around tower)

5 ¾" (14.6 cm)

3 ½" (8.9 cm)

8 ½" (21.6 cm)

Entrance
hole
1 ¼"
(3.2 cm)
diameter

9 ½" (24.1 cm)

2 ¾" (7 cm)

Base

15 ½" (39.4 cm)

Tower roof
side panel
(cut 2)
2" (5.1 cm)

Tower roof
end panel
(cut 2)
3" (7.6 cm)

Tower
roof top

9" (22.9 cm)

4 ½"
(11.4 cm)

4 ½"
(11.4 cm)

3" (7.6 cm)

2 ¾"
(7 cm)

3 ½"
(8.9 cm)

2" (5.1 cm)

Tower
side
panel
(cut 2,
1 with
entrance
hole)

9 ½" (24.1 cm)

2 ¾" (7 cm)

Birdhouse Plans

163

False Dovecote

MATERIALS

4′ (121.9 cm) square section of $\frac{1}{2}$″ (1.3 cm) thick exterior grade plywood

2′ (61 cm) square section of $\frac{1}{4}$″ (0.6 cm) plywood for internal partitions

Strips of 1 $\frac{1}{4}$″ x 1″ (3.2 cm x 2.5 cm) oak or softwood for edging

7′ (213.4 cm) oak board, approx. 7″ (17.8 cm) wide and 1″ (2.5 cm) thick

Softwood strips 1 $\frac{1}{2}$″ x 1″ (3.8 cm x 2.5 cm) for internal plywood section supports

1″ x $\frac{1}{4}$″ (2.5 cm x 0.6 cm) softwood strip for roof

2′ (61 cm) of $\frac{1}{2}$″ (0.6 cm) dowel

1 $\frac{1}{2}$″ (3.8 cm) screw

Brads

Sandpaper

Yellow glue

Wood preservative or gloss paint

TOOLS

Jigsaw

Handsaw

Web clamp

Hand plane

Try square

Tape measure and pencil

Screwdriver

Router or rabbet bit

Electric drill, drill bit

Hammer

Paintbrush

1. Cut the dovecote base from the plywood board following the template shown at right.

2. Make a smaller six-sided cutout, to act as a support for the oak side pieces.

3. Center and align the smaller piece, then screw it onto the base.

4. Either use ready-made solid wood moldings or form your own rabbet on the strip of 1 $\frac{1}{4}$″ x 1″ (3.2 cm x 2.5 cm) softwood. The rabbet should be the depth of the baseboard.

5. Cut the rabbeted strip into pieces longer than each side of the base and miter the ends, trimming until you have an exact fit.

6. Attach the edging to the board with brads and glue, flush with the underside of the base.

7. Drill drainage holes next to each point of the base, just inside the edging strips. Drill a further six holes nearer the center to allow any water that enters the dovecot to escape.

8. Cut the oak board into 11 $\frac{1}{2}$″ (29.2 cm) lengths for the sides. Plane the top of each side to 45° so that a smooth joint will be formed with the roof sections.

9. Plane the long edges of each oak side piece so that they fit around the smaller six-sided shape.

10. Form an entry hole in each piece of oak, three near the top and three at the bottom. Drill a large 1″ (2.5 cm) hole and two smaller holes just above. Then connect the three with a jigsaw.

11. Drill holes at the very bottom of each side so that the sides can be screwed to the small base support at a later stage.

12. Plane two edges of the 1 $\frac{1}{2}$″ x 1″ (3.8 cm x 2.5 cm) softwood strip and form a $\frac{1}{4}$″ (0.6 cm) rabbet down the center on the other face, to hold the plywood partitions.

13. Cut the finished strip into six pieces, slightly shorter than the oak sides.

14. Take each strip and drill two holes for screws at both the top and the bottom.

15. Assemble all the strips and side pieces, using glue and screws. Use a web clamp to hold all the pieces firmly until the glue has set.

16. Cut out the thinner plywood partitions to fit into the rabbets on the wood strips. In two of the partitions, cut slots halfway up their length in the center. Then slot these two partition pieces together and push them into the dovecote.

17. The remaining two narrower partition pieces can now be slid into position on each side of the slotted sections, completing the partitioning.

18. Cut out six triangular-shaped roof panels from the $\frac{1}{2}$″ (1.3 cm) plywood and plane the edges to fit together.

19. Screw and glue each piece to the top of the oak sides, using more glue between the section.

20. Cut the bottom roofing strips to length, mitering the ends so that they match the roof shape formed by the plywood. Decorate with random shallow saw cuts on one side, to simulate a shingle roof.

21. Attach the strips to the roof in slightly overlapping rows, cutting each piece so that it follows the line of the roof. Attach with glue and brads. Cut off the apex of the roof with a handsaw.

22. Next, make up a six-sided decorative piece from hardwood and bevel the top edges. Glue this to the top of the roof.

23. Drill $\frac{1}{2}$″ (1.3 cm) holes below each entrance hole and glue in dowel perches.

24. To form a shelter, jigsaw a bowed shape from scraps of the oak board and glue above the entrance holes.

25. Screw the dovecote to its base and plug the screw holes with solid wood. These should not be glued because you will need to open the dovecote for cleaning.

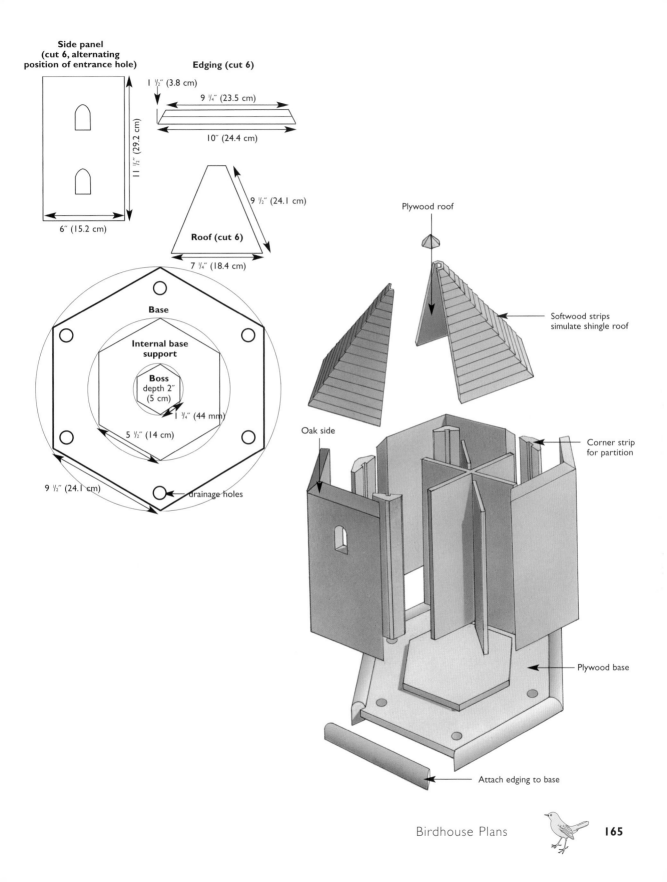

Side panel
(cut 6, alternating
position of entrance hole)

11 ½″ (29.2 cm)

6″ (15.2 cm)

Edging (cut 6)

1 ½″ (3.8 cm)

9 ¼″ (23.5 cm)

10″ (24.4 cm)

9 ½″ (24.1 cm)

Roof (cut 6)

7 ¼″ (18.4 cm)

Base

Internal base
support

Boss
depth 2″
(5 cm)

1 ¾″ (44 mm)

5 ½″ (14 cm)

9 ½″ (24.1 cm)

drainage holes

Plywood roof

Softwood strips
simulate shingle roof

Oak side

Corner strip
for partition

Plywood base

Attach edging to base

Houseboat

MATERIALS

20″ (50.8 cm) length of 10″ x 1″ (25.4 cm x 2.5 cm) planed pine

20″ (50.8 cm) length of 1″ (2.5 cm) square planed pine

10″ x 16″ (25.4 cm x 40.6 cm) piece of ³/₁₆″ (0.5 cm) thick birch-faced exterior grade plywood

20″ (50.8 cm) length of 4″ (10.2 cm) square planed pine

5′ (152.4 cm) length of ³/₄″ x 6″ (1.9 cm x 15.2 cm) planed pine

3″ (7.6 cm) length of ¹/₄″ (0.6 cm) diameter hardwood dowel

10′ (304.8 cm) length of rope (or plated chain)

1 ¹/₂″ (3.8 cm) brads

4 medium-sized plated eyebolts

Sandpaper

Piece of lightweight poster board

Yellow glue

Exterior grade clear varnish

10 No. 6 x 1 ¹/₄″ (3.2 cm) plated wood screws

TOOLS

Jigsaw

Backsaw

Electric drill (and drill stand if available)

Set of assorted twist drill bits

C-clamps

Pair of compasses

Coping saw

Rasp

Coarse rasp

Hammer

Bracing board

1 ¹/₂″ (3.8 cm) diameter holesaw

Screwdriver

Paintbrushes

Scissors

Plane

---

1. To make the deck, lay out two semicircles with a pair of compasses on either end of the piece of 10″ x 1″ (25.4 cm x 2.5 cm) pine so that the distance from end to end is 16″ (40.6 cm). Cut along the line with a jigsaw.

2. Using a scrap piece of wood as a guide (held in place with C-clamps), cut shallow grooves (⁷/₈″ (2.2 cm)) on the deck with a backsaw.

3. From the length of 1″ (2.5 cm) square pine, cut two pieces 8 ¹/₂″ (21.6 cm) long. Drill three countersunk holes in each ³/₁₆″ (0.5 cm) and attach them to the underside of the deck, ³/₁₆″ (.5 cm) from the edge, with glue and the No. 6 1 ¹/₄″ (3.2 cm) screws.

4. Cut a piece of ³/₁₆″ (0.5 cm) plywood to a width of 8 ¹/₂″ (21.6 cm) and a length of

13″ (33 cm). (Note that plywood will bend more easily one way than the other, so think carefully about the way that it is cut.) Glue and clamp one edge of the plywood to one side of the deck using a scrape piece of wood to distribute the pressure. Place some newspaper under the scrap wood to prevent it from sticking to the hull. Leave this to set for 24 hours.

5. Bend over the plywood to form the hull and glue this to the other side of the deck. You may need someone's assistance for this job—to apply the clamps while you bend the plywood.

6. From the length of 4″ square (10.2 cm) pine, cut two pieces 10″ (25.4 cm) long; with compasses mark a quadrant on both ends of each piece. Trim them to shape with a plane. Glue and clamp them to the front and back of the hull and leave overnight to set. These will form the bow and stern of the boat.

7. Using the profile of the deck as a guide, cut off the excess wood with a coping saw.

8. Finish the shaping process with a coarse rasp to achieve a quarter sphere

shape on either side of the hull. Make a template from a scrap piece of plywood that you can "offer up" to the nose as a shape tester. Cut away the nose until it is level with the plywood. Be careful not to cut into the plywood with the rasp. Remove rasp marks with medium grade grit sandpaper.

9. Lay out the profile of the rudder and bow on a piece of poster board and cut out with a pair of scissors. Using these as template, lay out the shapers on the 6″ x 1 ¹/₈″ (15.2 cm x 3.2 cm) pine. Cut out the profiles using the jigsaw fitted with a fine scrolling blade. Glue and nail the rudder and the bow to the hull.

10. On the remaining 6″ x ³/₄″ (15.2 cm x 0.6 cm) pine, lay out the sides and roof of the cabin. Cut these with a backsaw and a sawing board.

11. Using an electric drill and a holesaw, make a 1 ¹/₂″ (3.8 cm) entry hole for the birds in one of the cabin ends. A drill stand is not essential, but it helps. Clean the internal edge of the hole with sandpaper.

12. Assemble the cabin with glue and brads, and, when it is dry, trim any uneven surfaces with a plane.

13. Cut two lengths of wood scraps to a length of 4 ³/₈″ (11 cm). Drill two ³/₁₆″ (0.5 cm) countersunk holes in each and glue them to the inside base of the cabin. When the glue has set, attach the cabin to the deck with four No. 6 1 ¹/₄″ (3.2 cm) screws.

14. Using 1 ¹/₂″ (3.8 cm) brads and glue, attach the roof to the cabin.

15. Glue the tiller, made from ¹/₄″ (0.6 cm) dowel, into the predrilled hole on the rudder.

16. Sand off any remaining pencil or saw marks with medium grade grit sandpaper prior to varnishing. When the varnish has dried, sand with fine grain grit sandpaper, dust, and apply another coat of varnish. Repeat this process for a third application of varnish.

17. Drill ¹/₈″ (0.3 cm) pilot holes on the deck and screw in plated eyebolts. Attach rope or chain to the eyebolts so that you can suspend the birdhouse.

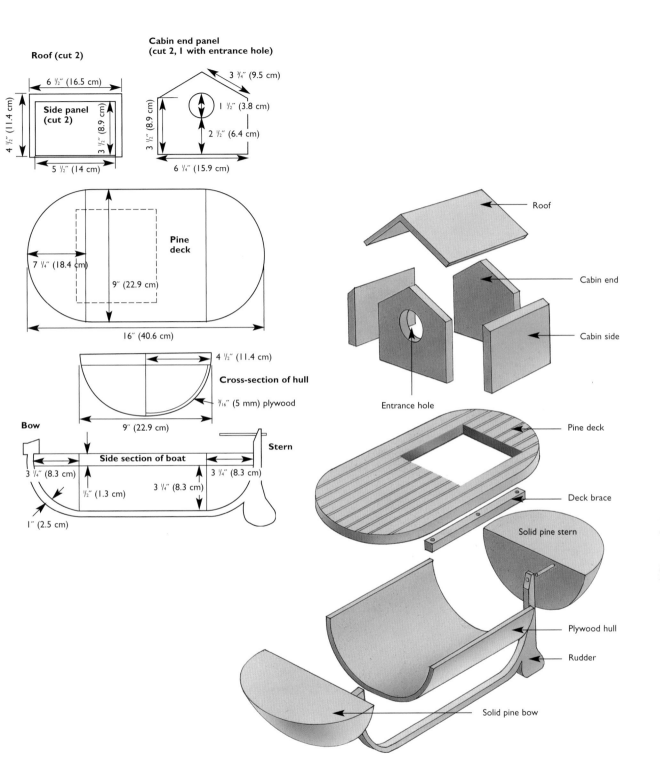

Roof (cut 2)

6 ½" (16.5 cm)

4 ½" (11.4 cm)

Side panel
(cut 2)

3 ½" (8.9 cm)

5 ½" (14 cm)

**Cabin end panel
(cut 2, 1 with entrance hole)**

3 ¾" (9.5 cm)

3 ½" (8.9 cm)

1 ½" (3.8 cm)

2 ½" (6.4 cm)

6 ¼" (15.9 cm)

Pine
deck

7 ¼" (18.4 cm)

9" (22.9 cm)

16" (40.6 cm)

4 ½" (11.4 cm)

Cross-section of hull

³⁄₁₆" (5 mm) plywood

9" (22.9 cm)

Bow

Stern

Side section of boat

3 ¼" (8.3 cm)

3 ¼" (8.3 cm)

½" (1.3 cm)

3 ¼" (8.3 cm)

1" (2.5 cm)

Roof

Cabin end

Cabin side

Entrance hole

Pine deck

Deck brace

Solid pine stern

Plywood hull

Rudder

Solid pine bow

City Bird

1. Using a handsaw, cut the softwood diagonally through its length and plane off any saw marks.

2. From the resultant triangular material, lay out and cut to a length of 24″ (61 cm) for the lower inner structure.

3. On the ¼″ (0.6 cm) MDF, lay out and cut with a jigsaw one piece 4 ¾″ × 24″ (12.1 cm × 61 cm) and one piece 4 ½″ × 24″ (11.4 cm × 61 cm). Trim to the line with a plane and then nail and glue these two pieces to the inner structure.

4. On the remaining piece of softwood, lay out half a pyramid, cut with a backsaw and plane off any saw marks; then glue this to the top of the inner structure.

5. From the piece of ¾″ (1.9 cm) MDF, mark and cut two lengths with a jigsaw and accurately plane to a width of 4 ¼″ (10.8 cm). Cut one piece to a length of 13″ (33 cm) and the other 17″ (43.2 cm). With a plane, bevel one end of both pieces to an angle of 45°, checking for accuracy with a sliding bevel or a miter square. Cut and accurately trim another two pieces of ¾″ (1.9 cm) MDF to 4 ¼″ × 2 ¼″ (10.8 cm × 5.7 cm). Glue and nail one to the end of the 13″ (33 cm) length of ¾″ (1.9 cm) MDF and the other 4″ (10.2 cm) up from the end of the other. These will form the rear structure and bottoms of the grain store.

6. Glue and nail the grain store structure to the main part of the bird feeder.

7. Lay out and cut the sides, fronts, and lids of the grain store from the ¼″ (0.6 cm) MDF; cut 45° angles on the side pieces.

8. Glue and nail these to the rear structure and bottoms of the grain stores.

9. From the remaining ¼″ (0.6 cm) MDF, cut two isosceles triangles with a base length of 4 ¾″ (12.1 cm) and other two sides of 9 ¾″ (24.8 cm). Trim the bases of

the triangles at an angle so that they fit accurately on the top of the skyscraper. When fitting is completed, glue and nail these to the top to form the roof of the feeder.

10. On the fronts of the feeders, lay out three rectangles with a craft knife. With an electric drill fitted with a ¾″ (1.9 cm) spade bit, drill out as much of the material as possible inside each rectangle.

11. Use a chisel and mallet to cut out the remainder of the MDF to knife line, so that the rectangles are accurate.

12. With the plane, bevel the top ends of the grain store fronts to correspond with the 45° angle of the sides.

13. Cut the wire mesh with wire cutters and staple this to the inside of the grain store fronts.

14. Glue and nail the grain store fronts in position.

15. Sand the feeder with medium grade grit sandpaper, removing any irregularities in the jointing and apply a coat of primer paint. When the primer has dried, sand with fine grade grit sandpaper and apply undercoat paint. Complete painting with a finishing color. Highlight windows and roofs with a darker, contrasting color.

16. Cut lengths of bike tire inner tube and staple it to the edges of the grain store lids/roofs.

17. In turn, staple the lids into position on the tops of the grain store to make a hinge.

18. With a pair of scissors, cut two yogurt cups at an angle of 45°, drill ⅛″ (0.3 cm) holes in the center of the base and then paint.

19. Mark the centers of the grain store lids/roofs and make indentations with an awl; screw two yogurt cups in position. Alternatively, cut a round hole in each roof and fit the pots in place.

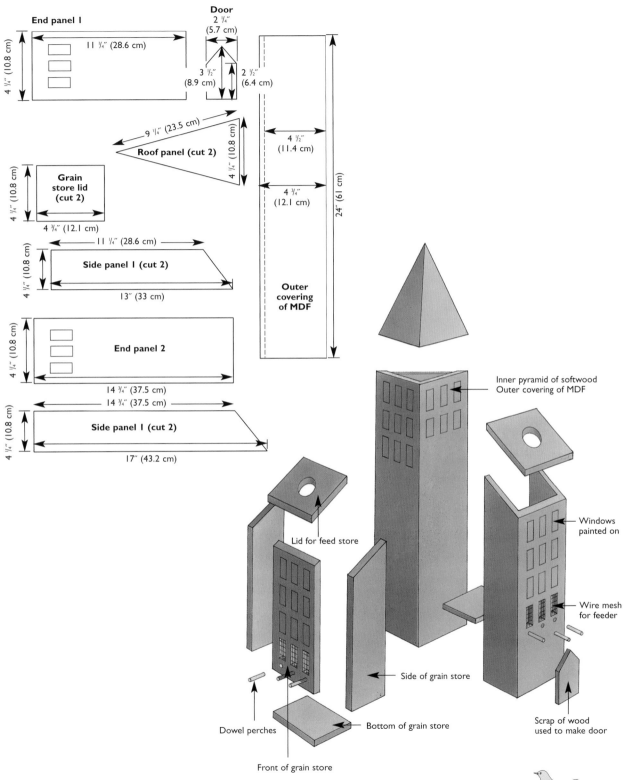

End panel 1

11 ¼" (28.6 cm)

4 ¼" (10.8 cm)

Door
2 ¼"
(5.7 cm)

3 ½"
(8.9 cm)

2 ½"
(6.4 cm)

9 ¼" (23.5 cm)

Roof panel (cut 2)

4 ¼" (10.8 cm)

4 ¼" (10.8 cm)

4 ½"
(11.4 cm)

4 ¾"
(12.1 cm)

24" (61 cm)

Grain store lid (cut 2)

4 ¼" (10.8 cm)

4 ¾" (12.1 cm)

Outer covering of MDF

11 ¼" (28.6 cm)

Side panel 1 (cut 2)

4 ¼" (10.8 cm)

13" (33 cm)

4 ¼" (10.8 cm)

End panel 2

14 ¾" (37.5 cm)

14 ¾" (37.5 cm)

4 ¼" (10.8 cm)

Side panel 1 (cut 2)

17" (43.2 cm)

Inner pyramid of softwood
Outer covering of MDF

Windows painted on

Wire mesh for feeder

Lid for feed store

Side of grain store

Scrap of wood used to make door

Dowel perches

Bottom of grain store

Front of grain store

169

Bird House Planter

MATERIALS

2 pieces cedar ⅞″ × 6″ × 12″
(2.2 cm × 15.2 cm × 30.5 cm)

2 piece plywood ⅜″ × 9 ½″ × 9 ½″
(1 cm × 24.1 cm × 24.1 cm)

1 piece plywood ⅜″ × 6 ¼″ × 9 ½″
(1 cm × 15.9 cm × 24.1 cm)

1 piece pine 1 ½″ × 3 ½″ × 9″
(3.8 cm × 8.9 cm × 22.9 cm)

1 piece cedar ⅞″ × 11 ¼″ × 11 ¼″
(2.2 cm × 28.6 cm × 28.6 cm)

2 pieces cedar ⅞″ × 2″ × 12″
(2.2 cm × 5.1 cm × 30.5 cm)

2 pieces cedar ⅞″ × 2″ × 13 ¾″
(2.2 cm × 5.1 cm × 34.9 cm)

Weatherproof wood glue

25 to 30 3D finishing nails

20 flathead nails, 2 ½″ (6.4 cm) long

Six 2″ (5.1 cm) deck screws

15 to 20 small 4″–5″ square
(10.2 cm–12.7 cm) scrap cedar or
asphalt roof shingles

Exterior paint or stain

Waterproof sealant or stain

4 six-packs of plants

Six to eight 3″ (7.6 cm) potted plants

Package of sheet moss

Liquid starter fertilizer

U-shape florist picks (optional)

Spanish moss for decoration

Water-soluble fertilizer

TOOLS

Table saw

Scissors

Pencil

Scroll saw

Drill and drill bit

Screwdriver

Hammer

Two buckets

1. Cut pieces with the table saw, and, as you go, check their fit. Make adjustments as necessary.

2. Make a pattern for triangular pieces A and B by copying the pattern to 215 percent on a copy machine. Cut out pattern; use it to draw lines for cutting scrollwork and entrance holes on A, aligning long edge of pattern with long edge of board. Cut triangular pieces A and B.

3. Using a scroll saw, cut bottom front edge of A along drawn line. Use a drill to cut a blade-start hole inside each marked entrance hole; cut the opening with the scroll saw.

4. Cut the plywood pieces C and D for the roof. Bevel-cut with table saw right side edge of C and left side edge of D at 45° angle to meet at the apex of the roof.

5. Apply a thin bead of weatherproof wood glue to seal beveled edges of roof at its apex; set triangular front and rear walls (A and B) under the roof as it dries to ensure proper fit for next step. Apply a line of glue all along the top edges of A and B. Use finishing nails to attach roof pieces C and D to A and B.

6. Cut E and F. Cut a rectangular notch in E (the floor) to accommodate the 2″ × 4″ (5.1 cm × 10.2 cm) mount F. Center the notch along the rear surface of the floor, where the 2″ × 4″ (5.1 cm × 10.2 cm) will extend through the floor and into the house. Drill four ⅜″ (1 cm) holes evenly spaced through the floor to allow for drainage. Position F so that 4″ (10.2 cm) of F is inside the house and 5″ (12.7 cm) of it extends from the bottom of the house. Attach F to B by driving deck screws through the back wall into F to secure the mount.

7. Install floor E; it should fit snugly to the mount. Position front wall A to the floor with the scrollwork just below the floor edge; use 3D finishing nails to nail front wall A into the edge of the floor. Nail E to inside of house using 3D finishing nail; nail through the front A and rear B into the edge of floor E.

8. Nail the cedar or asphalt shingles to the roof, allowing for overlap at the apex of the roof and slight overhang on the sides. If using cedar shingles, drill pilot holes in shingles, using a ³⁄₃₂″ (0.2 cm) drill bit, as a start for each nail hole to prevent splitting the shingles. Hammer 2 ½″ (6.4 cm) nails to the roof 2″ (5.1 cm) apart in staggered rows and jutting up 1″ (2.5 cm) for attaching the moss and plants later. (Repeat process for making pilot holes to prevent splitting cedar shingles, if using.)

9. Cut pieces G, H, and I. Cut eight drainage holes in G before nailing on side and rim pieces. Nail the 1″ × 2″ (2.5 cm × 5.1 cm) rim pieces H to the front and back edges of the base G, with the bottom edges flush. Repeat with side rim pieces I.

10. Center the house over the base and attach the base by screwing it to the bottom of mount F.

Front Wall Full-sized Pattern (A)

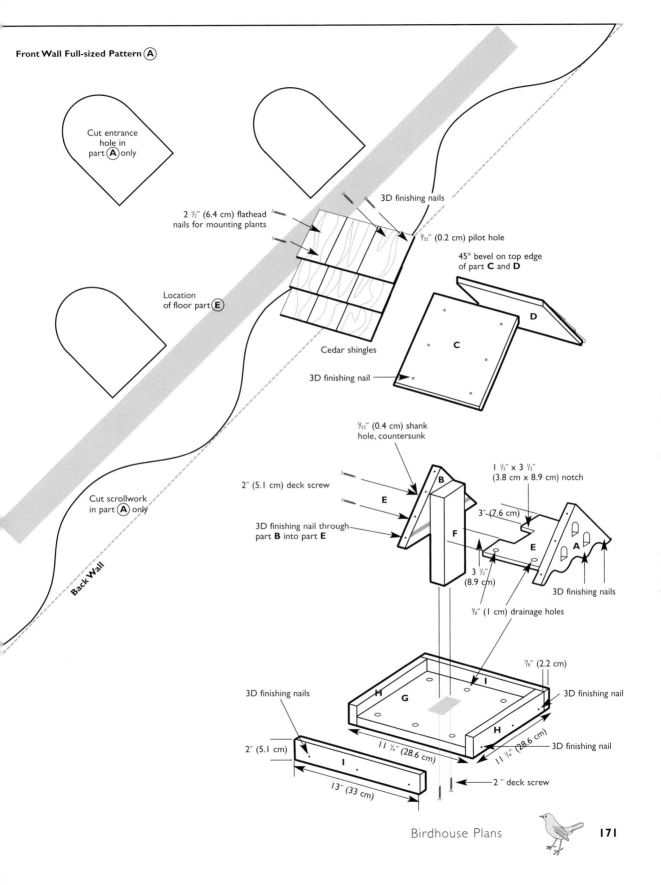

Cut entrance hole in part (A) only

2 ½″ (6.4 cm) flathead nails for mounting plants

3D finishing nails

⁹⁄₃₂″ (0.2 cm) pilot hole

45° bevel on top edge of part **C** and **D**

Location of floor part (E)

Cedar shingles

3D finishing nail

Cut scrollwork in part (A) only

Back Wall

⁵⁄₃₂″ (0.4 cm) shank hole, countersunk

2″ (5.1 cm) deck screw

3D finishing nail through part **B** into part **E**

1 ½″ x 3 ½″ (3.8 cm x 8.9 cm) notch

3″ (7.6 cm)

3 ½″ (8.9 cm)

⅜″ (1 cm) drainage holes

3D finishing nails

⅞″ (2.2 cm)

3D finishing nails

3D finishing nail

2″ (5.1 cm)

11 ¼″ (28.6 cm)

11 ¼″ (28.6 cm)

3D finishing nail

13″ (33 cm)

2 ″ deck screw

Arts and Crafts Birdhouse

MATERIALS

Graph paper

½" (1.3 cm) pine, 8′ × 5′
(2.4 m × 1.5 m)

¼" × 3" (0.6 cm × 7.6 cm)
eyebolt with flat washer and nut

Metal clip and wood screw

Wood glue

4D finishing nails

Sanding block

Medium-line sandpaper

Surfacing compound

Blue, green, and yellow acrylic paint

Clear satin polyurethane

TOOLS

Scissors

Tack cloth

Table saw

Jigsaw

Tape measure

Hammer

Nail set

Drill with ¼" (0.6 cm) and 1"
(2.5 cm) bits

1. Cut the pieces. Copy the pattern to scale on graph paper; cut out. Trace pattern onto wood. Use jigsaw to cut two pieces—one for the front and one for the back. Use table saw to cut down the middle of each piece. Sand bevel edges.

2. Use table saw to cut and rip two side pieces, two roof pieces, bottom pieces, perch, and six braces. Sand the edges of the two 5" (12.7 cm) braces to match the curve of the birdhouse front and back.

3. Use table saw to cut and rip four roof edge pieces. Use jigsaw to make the decorative half-moon cut on one roof edge piece, as shown. Blunt cut the bottom edge. Use it as a pattern for three remaining pieces. Set the table saw at 45° to cut the triangular roof brace.

4. Assemble the birdhouse. Glue and nail braces to front and back pieces. Drill entrance hole on front piece and air holes on back piece. Glue and nail perch. Align sides with front and back; glue and nail.

5. Glue and nail two roof pieces together, triangular roof brace to roof pieces, and roof edge pieces to roof. Drill a ¼" (0.6 cm) hole through roof and triangular brace; install eyebolt. Glue and nail roof to house. Install the metal clip with the wood screw. Insert bottom piece.

6. Finish the birdhouse. Set nails. Fill holes with surfacing compound. Sand; wipe with tack cloth. Paint the birdhouse body blue, the roof top and edges green, and the perch and the underside of the roof yellow; let dry. Top with polyurethane.

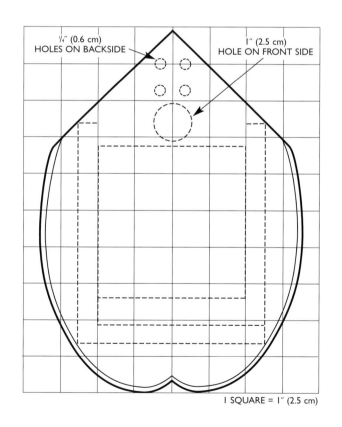

¼" (0.6 cm)
HOLES ON BACKSIDE

1" (2.5 cm)
HOLE ON FRONT SIDE

1 SQUARE = 1" (2.5 cm)

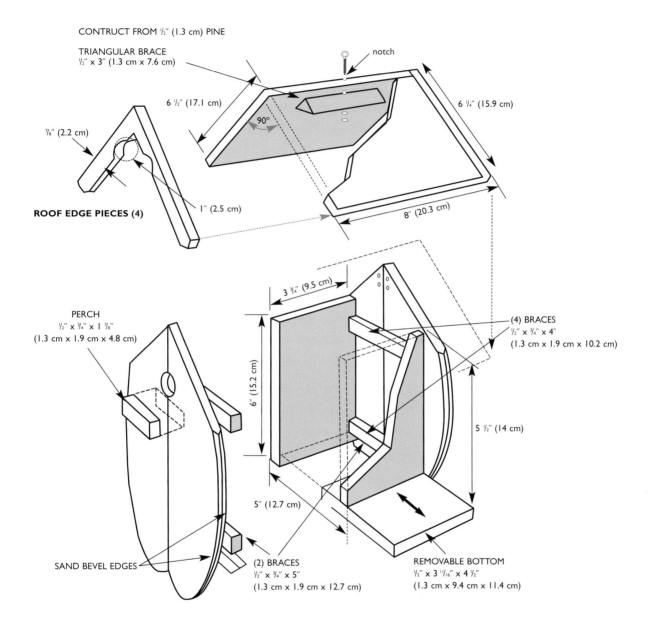

CONTRUCT FROM ½" (1.3 cm) PINE

TRIANGULAR BRACE
½" x 3" (1.3 cm x 7.6 cm)

notch

6 ½" (17.1 cm)

90°

7/8" (2.2 cm)

6 ¼" (15.9 cm)

ROOF EDGE PIECES (4)

1" (2.5 cm)

8" (20.3 cm)

3 ¾" (9.5 cm)

PERCH
½" x ¾" x 1 7/8"
(1.3 cm x 1.9 cm x 4.8 cm)

(4) BRACES
½" x ¾" x 4"
(1.3 cm x 1.9 cm x 10.2 cm)

6" (15.2 cm)

5 ½" (14 cm)

5" (12.7 cm)

SAND BEVEL EDGES

(2) BRACES
½" x ¾" x 5"
(1.3 cm x 1.9 cm x 12.7 cm)

REMOVABLE BOTTOM
½" x 3 11/16" x 4 ½"
(1.3 cm x 9.4 cm x 11.4 cm)

Recycled Garden Feeder

MATERIALS

1 piece of 12″ x 18″ x ⅜″
(30.5 cm x 45.7 cm x 1 cm) plywood

1 piece of 5″ x ¼″
(12.7 cm x 0.6 cm) diameter dowel

1 ¾″ (3.8 cm) panel pins

Screws

Stain/varnish

Old gardening tools, such as spade,
fork, or shovel

1. On ⅜″ (1 cm) plywood, draw a 10″ (25.4 cm) diameter disk around a suitable contain or lid. On one edge of the disk mark out a semicircular notch to fit around the tool's shaft.

2. Use a jigsaw to cut the circle out, after scoring along the line with a craft knife. Cut on the waste side of the line. Use abrasive paper with a sanding block to smooth the edges. Cut out the handle notch and finish the edge with abrasive paper wrapped around a piece of 1″ (2.5 cm) dowel.

3. Draw out on stiff paper the handle hook from our squared drawing. Each square represents 1″ (2.5 cm). Cut the shape out and the hook on the handle. Sand the edges with abrasive paper wrapped around a piece of 1″ (2.5 cm) dowel. Try it on the handle of your old garden tool and adjust the shape to suit.

4. Draw around the template onto ⅜″ (1 cm) plywood, score along the line, and cut out with a jigsaw. Sand the edges with abrasive paper wrapped around a piece of 1″ (2.5 cm) dowel.

5. Drill through the handle hook to take a 5″ (12.7 cm) length of ¼″ (0.6 cm) diameter dowel, ensuring prior to drilling that the drill size will produce a snug fit. Insert the dowel and drill a fine pilot hole through the edge of the plywood to take a long panel pin to secure it.

6. Drill two countersunk holes through the disk and screw the handle to it.

7. Paint the disk and handle hook with a water-based stain and/or varnish.

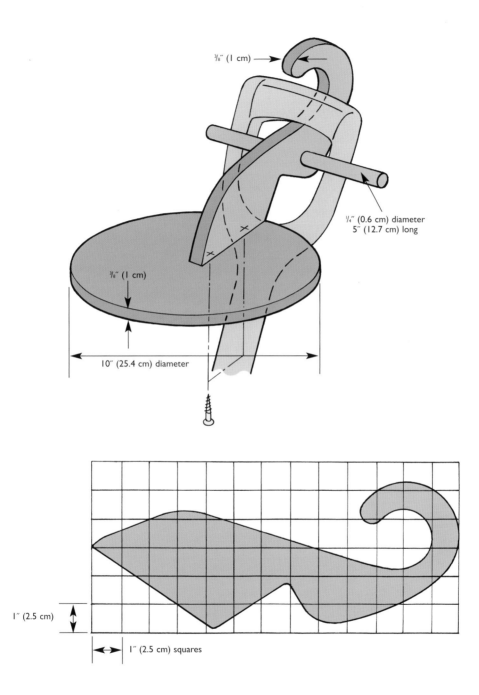

⅜″ (1 cm)

¼″ (0.6 cm) diameter
5″ (12.7 cm) long

⅜″ (1 cm)

10″ (25.4 cm) diameter

1″ (2.5 cm)

1″ (2.5 cm) squares

Chandelier Feeder

MATERIALS

1 piece of 30″ × 24″ × ⅜″
(76.2 cm × 61 cm × 1 cm) plywood

1 piece of 30″ × 1 ¼″
(76.2 cm × 3.2 cm) diameter dowel

1 piece of 40″ × 1″ × ⅜″
(101.6 cm × 2.5 cm × 1 cm) timber

Screws

Paint

1. On ⅜″ (1 cm) plywood, draw three disks of around 20″ (61 cm), 10″ (25.4 cm), and 7″ (17.8 cm) diameter, by drawing around suitable containers or lids.

2. You can make a simple beam compass from a 12″ (30.5 cm) length of 1″ × ¼″ (2.5 cm × 0.6 cm) batten. At one end of the batten mark a center point. Then measure from this, along the batten, other points at intervals of ½″ (1.3 cm). Through the first center point, drill a hole just large enough to grip a pencil. Counting from the pencil end, mark the center points at 3 ½″ (8.9 cm), 5″ (12.7 cm), and 10″ (25.4 cm). At each of these points, drill a fine pilot hole to grip a 1 ½″ (3.8 cm) panel pin.

3. Set the pin to the larger diameter. Dig the pin point lightly into the board and swing the compass to draw a complete circle. Reposition the pin and draw the other two circles. (You can then use the compass for other projects, drilling pin holes at appropriate intervals.)

4. Use a jigsaw to cut out the circles, after scoring along the line with a craft knife. Cut on the waste side of the line. Use abrasive paper with a sanding block to smooth the edges. Alternatively, use an electric router fitted with a trammel point for larger diameters, or trammel base for smaller ones. Using the router saves the need for excessive edge finishing.

5. At the center of each circle cut a 1 ¼″ (3.2 cm) diameter hole with a holesaw held in an electric drill.

6. On the larger table, screw four 8 ⅜″ (21.1 cm) length of 1″ × ⅜″ (2.5 cm × 1 cm) batten.

7. With either the jigsaw or router, cut three 4 ½″ (11.4 cm) circles. Cut each of them in half and drill two countersunk holes on the center line.

8. The post for the table is made in two parts: a square or round bottom section is drilled to take a 1 ¼″ (3.2 cm) diameter top section. Cut the top section to a length of 30″ (76.2 cm), round over the top and mark off the height of each table, starting at the bottom, at 8″ (20.3 cm), 10″ (25.4 cm), and 8″ (20.3 cm), and then leave 4″ (10.2 cm) at the top.

9. Drill each disk to take the half-round brackets on either side of the center hole. Slide the disks over the post to their position, and screw through the bracket into the post.

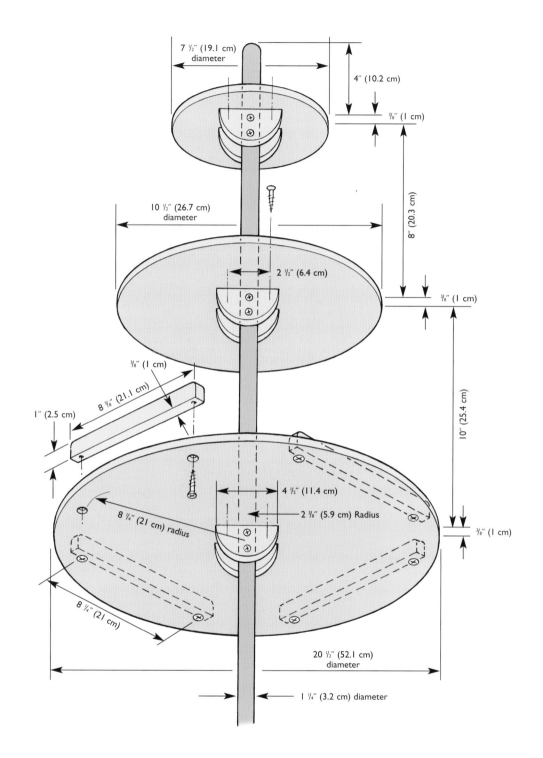

7 ½" (19.1 cm) diameter

4" (10.2 cm)

³⁄₈" (1 cm)

10 ½" (26.7 cm) diameter

8" (20.3 cm)

2 ½" (6.4 cm)

³⁄₈" (1 cm)

³⁄₈" (1 cm)

8 ³⁄₈" (21.1 cm)

1" (2.5 cm)

10" (25.4 cm)

4 ½" (11.4 cm)

2 ³⁄₈" (5.9 cm) Radius

8 ¼" (21 cm) radius

³⁄₈" (1 cm)

8 ¼" (21 cm)

20 ½" (52.1 cm) diameter

1 ¼" (3.2 cm) diameter

Birdhouse Plans

177

Patio Feeder

MATERIALS

One 48″ x 48″ (121.9 cm x 121.9 cm) sheet of ⅜″ (1 cm) plywood

1 piece of 7″ x 2″ x 2″ (17.8 cm x 5.1 cm x 5.1 cm) timber

1 ½″ (3.8 cm) thick square of hexagonal paving slab

48″ (121.9 cm) length of ½″ (1.3 cm) dowel

1 piece of 15″ x 6″ x ½″ (38.1 cm x 15.2 cm x 1.3 cm) plywood

Six 1″ (2.5 cm) x 12 gauge round-headed brass screws

Stain/varnish

Hanging nut feeder

OTHER TOOLS

Router fitted with straight bit and trammel bar

Beam compass

1. Draw the outline of the tree on a 48″ x 40″ (121.9 cm x 101.6 cm) sheet of ⅜″ (1 cm) plywood. Each section of the curved edge is a segment of a regular circle. Therefore, it can be drawn using a beam compass. Instructions for a simple beam compass can be found in the Chandelier Feeder project on page 162. For this project, counting from the pencil end, mark the center points at 5 ½″ (14 cm), 6″ (15.2 cm), and 8″ (20.3 cm). At each of these points, drill a fine pilot hole to grip a 1 ½″ (3.8 cm) panel pin.

2. Set out each center point on the board and set the compass to the appropriate diameter. Dig the pin point lightly into the board and swing the compass to draw a segment of a circle. Repeat this at each center point, crossing the ends of each segment.

3. Set out the trunk of the tree using freehand.

4. Score around the line with a craft knife, before cutting on the waste side (outside) of the line with a jigsaw. Make sure that the plywood is well supported and that the jigsaw cable is held clear of the saw cut. Finish the cut edges by sanding with abrasive paper wrapped over a sanding block.

FOOD AND WATER DISHES

5. Plastic or terra-cotta dishes for food and water are stood on round bases mounted through the board. The dishes we used were 14″ x 1 ½″ (35.6 cm x 3.8 cm) and 12″ x 1 ¾″ (30.5 cm x 4.4 cm). Mark out a horizontal slot, wide and long enough to slide the dish through. Add to the width ⅜″ (1 cm) to allow for the base thickness. Drill a hole in the waste area and score around the line at the curved ends. Insert the jigsaw blade through the hole and cut along the waste side of the line.

6. Using the router or a jigsaw, cut a circle with a diameter of 1″ (2.5 cm) more than the dish diameter. Similarly, cut a half-circle 2″ (5.1 cm) less than the base diameter. Cut the half-circle in half, glue and screw the two pieces either side of the board. Drill and countersink holes for this, offsetting them by the thickness of the plywood on opposite faces of the board to allow the screws to be inserted for the second piece after the first is fitted.

7. Drill and countersink the base after carefully positioning the hole centers over the brackets. Glue and screw the base onto the brackets.

8. Small containers for food or water can be mounted in a similar way as the table, but without cutting the slot through the board. Use a flat-sided base with a hole, less than the diameter of the container's rim, cut through it. Screw the base to a half-round bracket as before.

9. Hanging mesh feeders are available from most pet and garden supply stores. Measure the width and length of your feeder and add ¾″ (1.9 cm) to both. Set out these dimensions on the board. Use a small container to draw around for the curved ends. Drill a hole in the waste area, and score around the line at the curved ends. Insert the jigsaw blade through the hole and cut along the waste side of the line.

10. Seedcakes and sticks, fruit, and other tidbits can be hung on the board, either to the face or hanging within a cutout as for the feeder. Use round-headed brass screws for tying the food on.

11. Cut the perch to length from ½″ (1.3 cm) diameter dowel, but choose a drill size to ensure a tight fit when the dowel is inserted. Set out the center points and drill the dowel holes either cutting from both sides in turn or into waste material, to prevent the plywood breaking out on the rear face.

FINISHING TOUCHES

12. After filling any defects with epoxy filler, sand all surfaces smooth. Paint the tree with a water-based stain or varnish.

MOUNTING

13. Cut the 15″ x 6″ (38.1 cm x 15.2 cm) base from the ½″ (1.3 cm) plywood and screw a 7″ x 2″ x 2″ (17.8 cm x 5.1 cm x 5.1 cm) piece of wood to it. Drill the base to take two ⅜″ (1 cm) diameter bolts for fastening to a concrete paving slab. Insure that the bolts heads or nuts do not protrude below the underside of the slab: not only may they cause the tree to move, but they may also damage the roof or balcony surface. The tree may also be secured to an adjacent wall or fence post. Make up the wall bracket by screwing a half-disk of plywood to a wooden block. Plug and screw the block to the wall or screw it to a post. Attach the tree to the bracket using a bolt and wing nut to allow it to be detached easily.

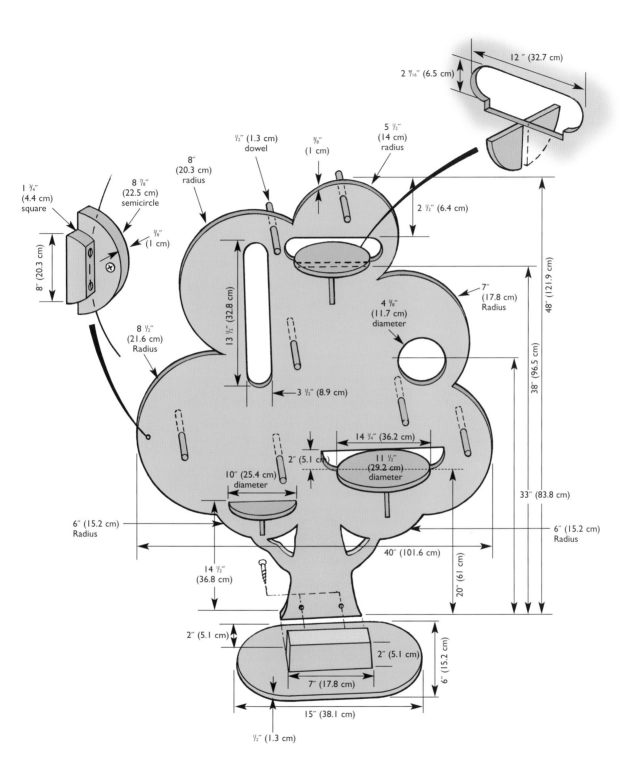

12 ″ (32.7 cm)

2 ⁹/₁₆″ (6.5 cm)

½″ (1.3 cm) dowel

⅜″ (1 cm)

5 ½″ (14 cm) radius

8″ (20.3 cm) radius

8 ⅞″ (22.5 cm) semicircle

1 ¾″ (4.4 cm) square

⅜″ (1 cm)

8″ (20.3 cm)

2 ½″ (6.4 cm)

8 ½″ (21.6 cm) Radius

13 ½″ (32.8 cm)

4 ⅝″ (11.7 cm) diameter

7″ (17.8 cm) Radius

48″ (121.9 cm)

38″ (96.5 cm)

3 ½″ (8.9 cm)

14 ¼″ (36.2 cm)

11 ½″ (29.2 cm) diameter

2″ (5.1 cm)

10″ (25.4 cm) diameter

6″ (15.2 cm) Radius

6″ (15.2 cm) Radius

33″ (83.8 cm)

40″ (101.6 cm)

20″ (61 cm)

14 ½″ (36.8 cm)

2″ (5.1 cm)

2″ (5.1 cm)

6″ (15.2 cm)

7″ (17.8 cm)

15″ (38.1 cm)

½″ (1.3 cm)

Birdhouse Plans **179**

Justina's Feeder

MATERIALS

I piece of 96″ x 2 ¼″ x ¾″
(243.8 cm x 5.7 cm, x 1.9 cm) timber

I piece of 24″ x 8″ x 1″ (61 cm x
20.3 cm 2.5 cm) timber (base)

I piece of 36″ x 1 ⅜″ x ¾″
(91.4 cm x 3.4 cm x 1.9 cm) timber

I piece of 36″ x 4″ x ¾″
(91.4 cm x 10.2 cm x 1.9 cm) timber

I piece of 3″ x 3″ x 9″
(7.6 cm x 7.6 cm x 22.9 cm) timber
(for turning finial and cap)

10′ (3 m) of ⅜″ (1 cm) link chain
(brass or stainless steel)

2 x ¾″ (1.9 cm) brass or stainless-steel
shackles (or stiff wire for making your
own)

Two 1 ½″ x ³⁄₁₆″ (0.5 cm) nuts and
bolts (brass or stainless steel)

6 brass or stainless-steel "S" hooks

2 dishes around 13″ (33 cm) diameter

1. Cut a length of 2 ¼″ x ¾″ (5.7 cm x 1.9 cm) wood into length of 5″ (12.7 cm), 23″ (58.4 cm), 34″ (86.4 cm), and 34″ (86.4 cm).

2. Glue the two shorter pieces between the two larger ones, leaving the exact size of sockets for the beam and pan support, and clamp until dry.

3. Plane the sides of the pillar square. From the base and beam socket, mark out the length of the side moldings.

4. Using an electric router fitted with a self-guiding "ovolo" router bit, cut along each edge in turn; then cut each edge, running the router on the adjacent face. This is to cut the same detail at the end of the molding on both faces. To do this, the router bit must be set accurately, so cut several test pieces on waste material to ensure that it is correct. Alternatively, a 45° chamfer can be cut with a spokeshave.

5. Draw the beam shape on 4″ x ¾″ (10.2 cm x 1.9 cm) piece, and cut it out as accurately as possible with a jigsaw. Plane and sand the edges straight and square.

6. Cut a chamfer around the edges of the beam using either a spokeshave or the electric router fitted with a self-guiding, 45° chamfer routing bit.

7. Glue the beam in the socket and secure with two screws.

8. Cut the lower pan support from a piece of 1 ⅜″ x ¾″ (3.4 cm x 1.9 cm) wood and chamfer the edges as before. Glue the support in the socket and secure with two screws. At the end of each arm, screw a 2″ (5.1 cm) diameter wooden pad.

9. The base is made up of three 8″ x 8″ x 1″ (20.3 cm x 20.3 cm x 2.5 cm) pieces. Alternate the grain direction and glue and clamp the blocks until dry. Plane a 45° chamfer along each edge.

10. The pillar is fitted into a mortise cut in the center of the base. Mark out the size of the mortise, equal to the finished size of the pillar. Drill several large-diameter holes to remove most of the waste before squaring the mortise with a chisel. Glue the pillar into the mortise and secure with a screw from beneath.

FINIALS

11. Turn the top finial on a lathe, leaving a ¼″ x 1″ (0.6 cm x 2.5 cm) diameter spigot for gluing into the cap. Turn the cap on the lathe or cut it square, leaving a 1″ (2.5 cm) diameter socket in the center. Glue and screw the cap onto the top of the pillar and glue the finial into it. Alternatively, use a turned wooden door knob you've bought from the hardware store.

12. Drill through the rim of two 13″ (33 cm) diameter plastic dishes to take three equally spaced S hooks. Position the dishes on the pads and measure the length of the chains to the beam, leaving a couple of extra links. Bend a stiff piece of brass or galvanized wire to form a shackle for the chains, fitting the chains before bending the second eye. Drill through the center of the beam ends and bolt through the shackles. Adjust the length of the chains by removing spare links as necessary. Drill one hole through the bottom of the dish and use a small round-headed screw to fasten it to the pad. Drainage holes can be drilled in the bottom of the dishes to stop them from filling with rain. For use as a bird bath, use a third dish placed on one of the fished dishes.

FINISHING TOUCHES

13. The scales can be mounted on a brick pier of similar dimensions to the base or larger, fitting a capping stone between the two. To secure it, screw two or more long wood screws partway into the underside of the base, and set them into mortar-filled joints or holes in the pier.

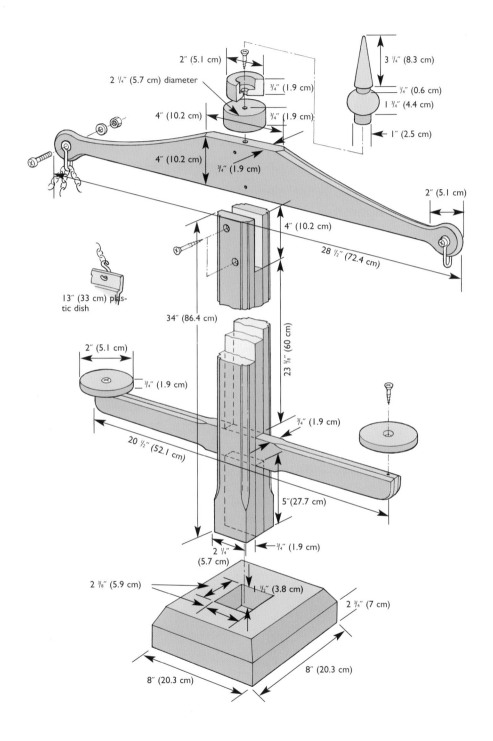

2″ (5.1 cm)

2 ¼″ (5.7 cm) diameter

¾″ (1.9 cm)

4″ (10.2 cm)

¾″ (1.9 cm)

3 ¼″ (8.3 cm)

¼″ (0.6 cm)

1 ¾″ (4.4 cm)

1″ (2.5 cm)

4″ (10.2 cm)

¾″ (1.9 cm)

2″ (5.1 cm)

13″ (33 cm) plastic dish

4″ (10.2 cm)

28 ½″ (72.4 cm)

34″ (86.4 cm)

2″ (5.1 cm)

¾″ (1.9 cm)

23 ⅝″ (60 cm)

¾″ (1.9 cm)

20 ½″ (52.1 cm)

5″ (27.7 cm)

2 ¼″ (5.7 cm)

¾″ (1.9 cm)

2 ⅜″ (5.9 cm)

1 ½″ (3.8 cm)

2 ¾″ (7 cm)

8″ (20.3 cm)

8″ (20.3 cm)

Time to Eat

MATERIALS

1 piece of 24″ x 18″ x ½″
(61 cm x 45.7 cm x 1.3 cm) plywood

1 piece of 24″ x 1 ¼″ x 1 ¼″
(61 cm x 3.2 cm x 3.2 cm) timber

1 piece of 48″ x 48″ x ⅜″
(121.9 cm x 121.9 cm x 1 cm) plywood

1 piece of 48″ x ⅜″
(121.9 cm x 1 cm) half-round bead

1 piece of 8″ x ⅝″ x 1″
(20.3 cm x 1.6 cm x 2.5 cm) timber

1 piece of 36″ x 3 ⅛″ x ¾″
(91.4 cm x 7.9 cm x 1.9 cm) timber

Exterior wood glue

Screws

Stain and paint

¾″ (1.9 cm) molding pins

4 ½″ (11.4 cm) square of clear Perspex

4 ½″ (11.4 cm) square of
white laminate

Quartz clock movement

OTHER TOOLS

³⁄₁₆″ (0.5 cm) dowel bit

Beam compass

ROOF

1. Draw the four triangular roof segments (base 16″ (40.6 cm) x height 12 ½″ (31.8 cm)) on a piece of ⅜″ (1 cm) plywood with the grain running along their length and the wide and narrow ends alternated. Leave a gap of ⅛″ (0.3 cm) between each to allow for the width of the saw blade. Score across the grain along the angled edges before cutting.

2. Cut out each segment and mark one face of each. (This will be the inside face when the segments are glued together.) Stack all four segments together in a vise, and plane all to the same size with all the edges square.

3. On the opposite edges of two of the segments, mark an angle of 60° and join the lower points with a line drawn parallel to the edge. The actual finished angled will be slightly greater, but this will provide a good guide to work to.

4. Bevel the edges of the two segments by planing down to the line, taking care not the decrease the width of each piece. Check and adjust the angle by lightly planing until their faces mate along their full length when their bases are set at an angle of 90°. Set a bevel gauge to the finished edge angle and mark and plane the remaining segment edges to this angle.

5. Glue and pin the four segments together. To hold the roof square while drying, pin two battens at 90° onto a piece of waste board and push the roof against them. Pin two further battens against the remaining two edges and pin these securely.

6. Cut a square panel of ⅜″ (1 cm) plywood to fit into the underside of the roof ⅜″ (1 cm) above the bottom edge. Draw lines parallel to and ⅜″ (1 cm) in from each edge on one face of the panel. Plane down to the line to leave an angle of 45° around the edge. Glue and pin the panel into the base of the roof.

7. When completely dry, plane or sand the bottom edges straight and square and finish the vertical joints of the roof flush.

PILLARS

8. Cut four 1 ½″ x 1 ¼″ x 5″ (3.2 cm x 3.2 cm x 12.7 cm) pillars. Drill a hole centrally in one end of each to a ³⁄₁₆″ (0.5 cm) dowel.

9. On the underside of the roof, mark out the position of the pillars—leaving a dimension of 8 ¼″ (21 cm) between each—and mark the center point of each pillar. Drill a ³⁄₁₆″ (0.5 cm) hole at each point to take the dowels. Apply glue to the top of the pillar and the dowels and glue the pillars in place, square to the baseboard sides, using masking tape to hold them in place and square until dry.

BRACKETS

10. Draw out the shape of one bracket on a piece of ³⁄₁₆″ (1 cm) plywood. Score the curved line and cut the bracket out. Smooth the edges with a file and/or abrasive paper.

11. Use the first bracket as a template for drawing the seven remaining ones. Cut and finish all the brackets and drill a fine pilot hole to take the fixing pins. Glue and pin each bracket to the pillars and roof.

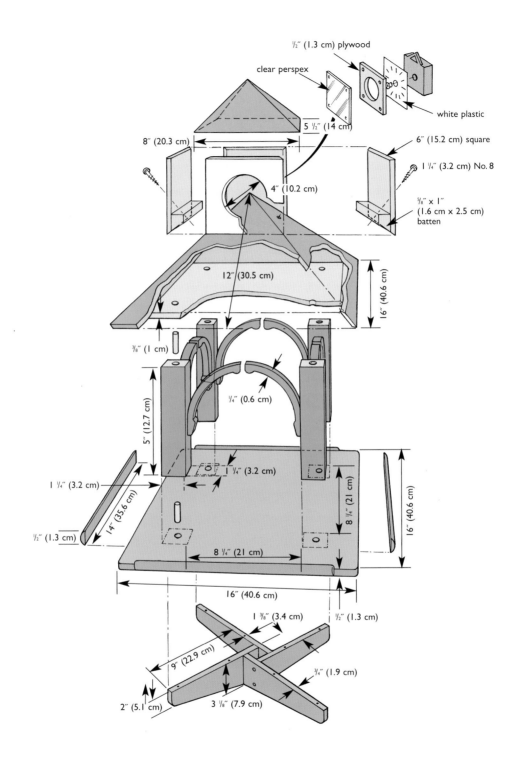

½" (1.3 cm) plywood

clear perspex

5 ½" (14 cm)

8" (20.3 cm)

4" (10.2 cm)

white plastic

6" (15.2 cm) square

1 ¼" (3.2 cm) No. 8

⅝" x 1"
(1.6 cm x 2.5 cm)
batten

12" (30.5 cm)

16" (40.6 cm)

⅜" (1 cm)

¼" (0.6 cm)

5" (12.7 cm)

1 ¼" (3.2 cm)

8 ¼" (21 cm)

16" (40.6 cm)

1 ¼" (3.2 cm)

14" (35.6 cm)

½" (1.3 cm)

8 ¼" (21 cm)

16" (40.6 cm)

1 ⅜" (3.4 cm)

½" (1.3 cm)

9" (22.9 cm)

¾" (1.9 cm)

2" (5.1 cm)

3 ⅛" (7.9 cm)

Time to Eat (continued)

CLOCKTOWER

12. Cut four 8″ x 5 ½″ (20.3 cm x 14 cm) triangular segments from ⅜″ (1 cm) plywood and make up the small roof in a similar fashion to the main roof, planing the joint face angles, but omitting the square panel.

13. Cut four 6″ (15.2 cm) square ⅜″ (1 cm) plywood side pieces and mark the inside face. Plane a 45° miter along two opposite edges on the marked face of each. Plane a 60° angle on the opposite faces of the other two edges.

14. Use a pair of compasses to mark out a 4″ (10.2 cm) circle in the center of one panel. With a router or jigsaw, cut out the circle, finishing the edges with abrasive paper wrapped over a curved block.

15. Glue and pin the four sides together and check for squareness. Glue and pin the roof to the mitered edge of the walls.

16. Cut an 8″ (20.3 cm) length of ⅝″ x 1″ (1.6 cm x 2.5 cm) batten and plane one face to an angle of 45°. Cut the batten into two pieces and glue them to the inside bottom edges of two opposite sides, the beveled face being flush to the beveled face of the batten.

17. Drill neat countersunk holes through the side panels and battens to take 1 ¼″ (3.2 cm) x 8 gauge brass screws. Stand the clocktower on the roof and drill pilot holes to position the holding-down screws.

18. Quartz clock movements and hands can be bought quite inexpensively from most craft supplies outlets. Cut a 4 ½″ x 4 ½″ (11.4 cm 11.4 cm) square of white plastic and drill the center to take the threaded tube of the movement. Set out the clock face on this piece using black acrylic paint or self-adhesive numbers. Cut a 4 ½″ x 4 ½″ (11.4 cm 11.4 cm) square of clear Perspex or other transparent sheet.

19. Mark out a 4 ½″ x 4 ½″ (11.4 cm 11.4 cm) square of ½″ (1.3 cm) plywood and draw a 4″ (10.2 cm) circle in the center. In the center of the square cut a 4″ (10.2) diameter circle as before. Cut out the square and clamp all three pieces in a vise, lining up their edges. Drill a ¹⁄₁₆″ (0.2 cm) diameter circle in each corner, through all three pieces. Use these holes to mount the movement, using ⅜″ (1 cm) round-headed brass screws. (Fit the battery and set the clock to the correct time before mounting the clock housing to the main roof, when the finished bird table is positioned outdoors.)

20. After filling any defects and pin holes (do not fill over the heads of the two mounting screws), sand all surfaces smooth. Paint the roof and walls with exterior masonry paint.

BASEBOARD AND MOUNTING BRACKET

21. Cut the 16″ x 16″ (40.6 cm x 40.6 cm) baseboard from ½″ (1.3 cm) plywood and plane the edges straight and square.

22. Cut four 14″ x 14″ (35.6 cm x 35.6 cm) lengths of 1″ (2.5 cm) half-round bead, plane a narrow flat along the edges, and round the ends. Glue and pin the beads to the edge of the baseboard.

23. Draw around a coin to mark the radiused cornered. Score around the line before cutting with a jigsaw and sanding to a smooth curve.

24. Mark out and cut the four support brackets from a piece of ¾″ (1.9 cm) wood. Screw the four pieces together and position them on the underside of the baseboard. Drill through the baseboard and glue and screw the battens to the underside.

FINISHING TOUCHES

25. After filling any defects and recessed pin and screw heads with epoxy filler, sand all surfaces smooth. Paint the roof with exterior masonry paint. Paint both the baseboard and pillars with a suitable nontoxic, exterior-grade varnish or stain.

PHOTO CREDITS

SOURCES

. . . .

Craftspeople/Designers

Cary and Janice Bills
Route 5, Box 78
Lewisburg, TN 37091
(615) 276-2306
Architectural birdhouses with a
"vintage" look.

Mary Donald Inc.
457 Schoolhouse Lane
Devon, PA 19333
(215) 293-1441
Decoratively painted
birdhouses.

Laura Foreman
(212) 227-9067
One-of-a-kind, highly
original birdhouses.

Garden Source Furnishings
200 Bennet Street
Atlanta, GA 30309
(404) 351-6446
Folk-art-inspired architectural
birdhouses.

Larry Kenosha
Bright Development Services
1010 West Brook Way
Hopkins, MN 55343
(612) 938-6178
Log cabin-style birdhouse
crafted of Minnesota materials.

Barry Leader
Arts for the Birds
122 West High Street
Elizabethtown, PA 17022
(717) 367-2990
Whimsical painted-wood
birdhouses.

Clifton Monteith
P.O. Box 9
Lake Ann, MI 49650
(616) 275-6560
Elegant hand-crafted wood and
bent-twig birdhouses.

Randy Ouzts
P.O. Box 261
Belmont, NC 28012
(704) 825-3046
Birdhouses and feeders crafted
from wood, kudzu, and other
vines.

Michael Ridel
The Wood Shed
12169 Greenock Lane
Los Angeles, CA 90049
(213) 658-4519
Detailed architectural
birdhouses.

Randy Sewell
38 Muscogee Avenue N.W.
Atlanta, GA 30305
(404) 239-9130
Painted-wood architectural
birdhouses inspired by vintage
American roadside architecture.

The Streck Family
805 D Early Street
Santa Fe, NM 87501
(505) 984-8265
Southwestern-style painted-
wood birdhouses with tin and
copper details.

Nancy Thomas Studio Gallery
P.O. Box 274
Yorktown, VA
Decoratively painted
birdhouses.

Manufacturers/Distributors

*The making of birdhouses is, in gen-
eral, a cottage industry, and the
distinction between craftspeople and
manufacturers is often slight. Many of
the firms listed below employ or are
owned by talented artisans, and most
of their birdhouses are hand-crafted.*

Added Oomph
P.O. Box 6135
High Point, NC 27262
(919) 886-4410
Spectacular fiberglass birdhouse
in the shape of a garden folly.

Back Shore Woodworks
P.O. Box 33
Chamberlain, ME 04541
(207) 677-3625
Decorative, bird-friendly
birdhouses and feeders.

Bird Buddies
4005 Crawford Road
Spicewood, TX 78669
(800) 621-8407
Decorative rustic-style
birdhouses and feeders.

Country Originals
3844 West Northside Drive
Jackson, MS 39209
(601) 366-4229
Fanciful wood and tin
birdhouses; bee skep birdhouse..

English Thatch
P.O. Box 130287
Houston, TX 77219
(713) 524-7415
Thatched-roof birdhouses

Lady Slipper Designs
Route 3, Box 556
Bemidji, MN 56601
White painted-wood birdhouses
in a variety of architectural
styles. Write for list of retailers.

Lazy Hill Farms
P.O. Box 235
Colerain, NC 27924
(919) 356-2828
Cedar and cypress birdhouses
and feeders in traditional styles,
including shingle-roofed
English dovecotes.

Milano Series
(914) 699-3050
Modern and Postmodern
architectural birdhouses.

Remington Freeman Ltd.
225 Fifth Avenue
New York, NY 10010
(212) 689-5542
Distributors of a variety of
rustic and other birdhouses.

Terra Cotta Creations
Route 2, Box 160
Nixa, MO 65714
(417) 725-1108
Terra-cotta birdhouses.

Retailers

*Because of their popularity and col-
lectibility, birdhouses can be found in
an increasing number of shops and
galleries—even department stores.
The list below is by its nature selec-
tive. Don't hesitate to investigate
retailers in your area, particularly*
*home-design emporia, country stores,
and garden-furnishings shops.*

ABC Carpet & Home
888 Broadway
New York, NY 10003
(212) 473-3000
Birdhouses in a variety of styles.

American Primitive Gallery
596 Broadway, Suite 205
New York, NY 10012
(212) 966-1530
Extensive selection of vintage
and new folk-art birdhouses.

Birdnest of Ridgefield
2 Big Shop Lane
Ridgefield, CT 06877
(203) 431-9889
Anything related to wild
birding, including new and
vintage birdhouses.

Birdwatchers General Store
36 Route 6A
Orleans, MA 02653
(508) 255-6974
Wide selection of bird-friendly
houses and feeders.

Cherishables
1608 20th Street N.W.
Washington, DC 20009
(202) 785-3616
Miniature birdhouse ornaments.

Crow's Nest Birding Shop
Cornell Laboratory of
Ornithology
159 Sapsucker Woods Road
Ithaca, NY 14850
(607) 254-2400

Nesting boxes and shelves,
finished or in kit form.

Dovetails
511 East Water Street
Charlottesville, VA 22901
(804) 979-9955
Vintage birdhouses.

Flights of Fancy
450 East 78th Street
New York, NY 10021
(212) 772-1302
Decorative rustic birdhouses
and feeders.

Growingthings
81-A Seventh Avenue
Brooklyn, NY 11217
(718) 638-0918
Wildly ornamented rustic-style
birdhouses.

Lexington Gardens
1008 Lexington Avenue
New York, NY 10021
(212) 861-4390
Decorative birdhouses.

Massachusetts Audubon Shop
South Great Road
Lincoln, MA 01773
(617) 259-9661
Houses, kits, and nesting
shelves for eleven species.

The Sampler
96 Summit Avenue
Summit, NJ 07901
(908) 277-4747
Wide selection of decorative
birdhouses, and a display of
vintage birdhouses.

Shapiro and Stambaugh
Eighth Alley
Newmarket, MD 21774
(301) 865-5027
Interesting selection of vintage
birdhouses.

Wild Goose Chase
1631 Sunflower Avenue
Santa Ana, CA 92704
(714) 966-2722
Good selection of vintage folk-
art birdhouses. (See their next-
door shop, Sweet William, for
newer houses.)

Zona
97 Greene Street
New York, NY 10021
(212) 925-6750
Unusual rustic-style birdhouses.

Catalogues/Mail Order

*A growing number of catalogues offer
birdhouses and feeders by mail, but
because their merchandise varies from
season to season, they have not been
included here. The catalogues listed
below are distinguished by their
unique selections.*

Kinsman Company, Inc.
River Road
Point Pleasant, PA 18950
(215) 297-5613
(800) 733-5613
German "wood-crete" bird-
houses, open swallow boxes.

Plow & Hearth
301 Madison Road
Orange, VA 22960
(800) 627-1712
Bluebird, wren, and bat houses,
robin shelves, swallow nesting
dishes, and predator guards.

Winterthur Gift & Garden
Sampler
Winterthur Museum and
Gardens
Dover, DE 19901
(800) 767-0500
Decorative wood and terra-cotta
birdhouses, including replicas of
the bluebird houses found in the
gardens at Winterthur.

Organizations

*In addition to the organizations listed
below, local Audubon Society chap-*

*ters can provide information on bird-
houses and bird housing.*

Bat Conservation International
P.O. Box 162603
Austin, TX 78716
This nonprofit organization is
dedicated to reversing the severe
decline in bat populations.

National Wildlife Federation
1400 16th Street, N.W.
Washington, DC 20036
The federation's Backyard
Wildlife Habitat Program shows
homeowners how to attract
birds and other wildlife by
providing food and cover.

North American Bluebird
Society
P.O. Box 6295
Silver Spring, MD 20916
The society has been responsible
for helping to preserve
America's precious and
threatened bluebirds. Write for
information on bluebird
preservation or to order houses
for eastern and western
bluebirds.

BIBLIOGRAPHY

Buff, Sheila. *The Birder's Catalogue*. New York: Simon & Schuster, 1989.

Cosgrove, Irene. *My Recipes Are for the Birds*. New York: Doubleday, 1976.

Davison, Verne E. *Attracting Birds*. New York: Thomas Y. Crowell, 1967.

DeGraaf, Richard M., and Gretchin M. Witman. *Trees, Shrubs, and Vines for Attracting Birds*. Amherst, MA: University of Massachusetts Press, 1979.

Dennis, John V. *A Complete Guide to Bird Feeding*. New York: Alfred A. Knopf, 1975.

Harrison, George H. *The Backyard Bird Watcher*. New York: Simon & Schuster, 1979.

Henderson, Carol L. *Woodworking for Wildlife*. St. Paul, MN: Minnesota Department of Natural Resources, 1984.

Kress, Stephen W. *The Audubon Society Guide to Attracting Birds*. New York: Charles Scribner's Sons, 1985.

————. *The Audubon Society Handbook for Birders*. New York: Charles Scribner's Sons, 1981.

McNeil, Don. *The Birdhouse Book*. Seattle: Pacific Search Press, 1979.

Schultz, Walter E. *How to Attract, House and Feed Birds*. New York: Macmillan, 1970.

Stokes, Donald and Lillian. *The Bird Feeder Book*. Boston: Little, Brown, 1988.

————. *The Complete Birdhouse Book*. Boston: Little, Brown, 1990.

Terres, John K. *Songbirds in Your Garden*. New York: Hawthorn Books, 1977.

Wade, J. L. *Attracting Purple Martins*. Griggsville, IL: Nature Society, 1987.

Weber, Dorothy Fitzcharles. *Artistry in Avian Abodes: The Little Birdhouse Book*. Williamsburg, VA: Williamsburg Publishing.

Wells, Malcolm. *Classic Architectural Birdhouses and Feeders*. Brewster, MA: 1989. (Because the book is self-published, it can most easily be obtained from the author, at 673 Satucket Road, Brewster, MA 02631).